# LITTLE BOOK OF HORROR™
## FRANKENSTEIN

IDW

SAN DIEGO, CA

Lettering and Design by Robbie Robbins

Edited by Chris Ryall

Inspired by Mary Shelley's *Frankenstein*

www.idwpublishing.com

IDW Publishing is:
Ted Adams, Publisher
Chris Ryall, Editor-in-Chief
Robbie Robbins, Design Director
Kris Oprisko, Vice President
Alex Garner, Art Director
Cindy Chapman, Operations Manager
Tom B. Long, Designer
Chance Boren, Editorial Assistant
Aaron Myers, Editorial Assistant
Yumiko Miyano, Business Development
Rick Privman, Business Development

# LITTLE BOOK OF HORROR™
## FRANKENSTEIN

WRITTEN BY

# STEVE NILES

PAINTED ART BY

# SCOTT MORSE

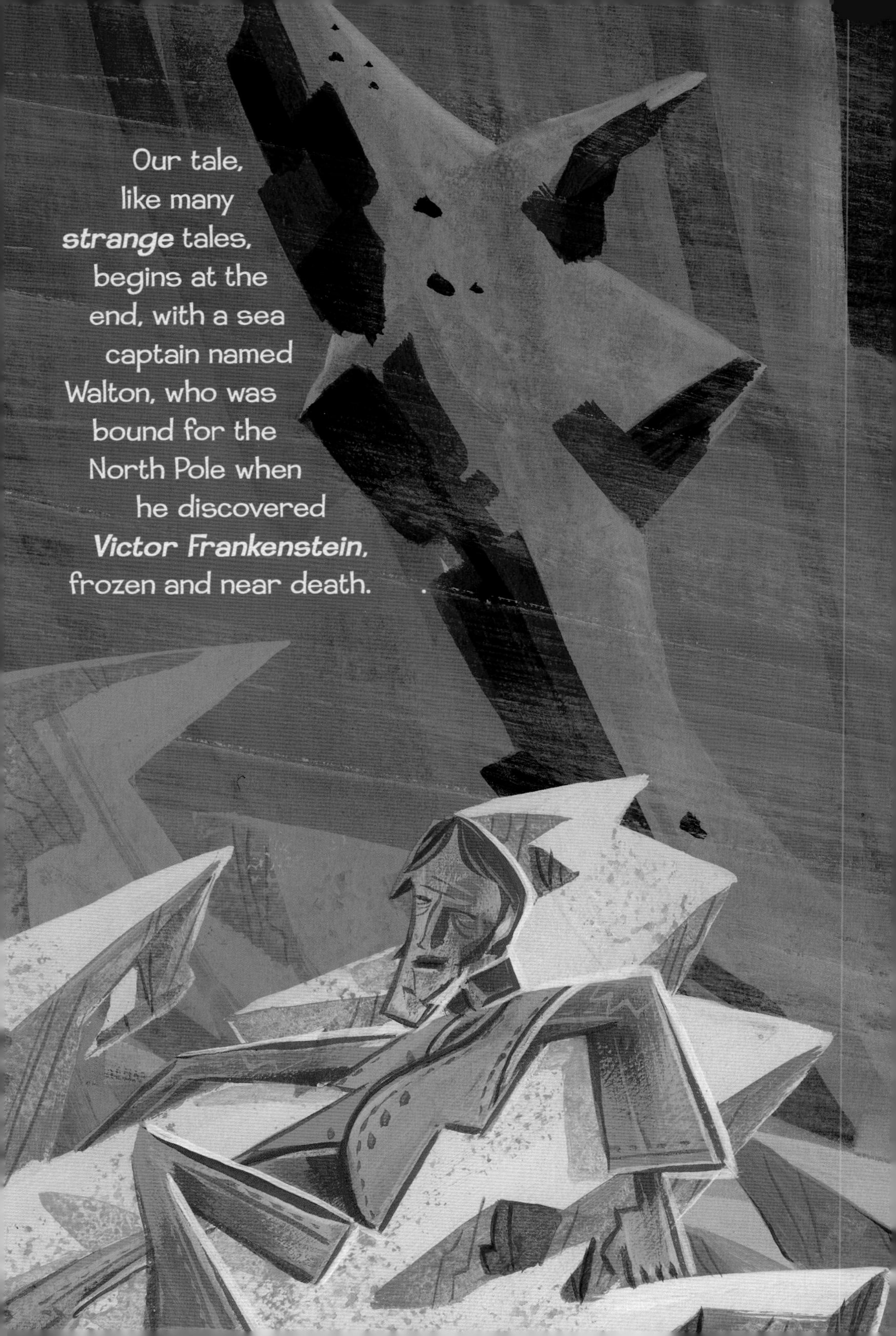

Our tale, like many ***strange*** tales, begins at the end, with a sea captain named Walton, who was bound for the North Pole when he discovered ***Victor Frankenstein,*** frozen and near death.

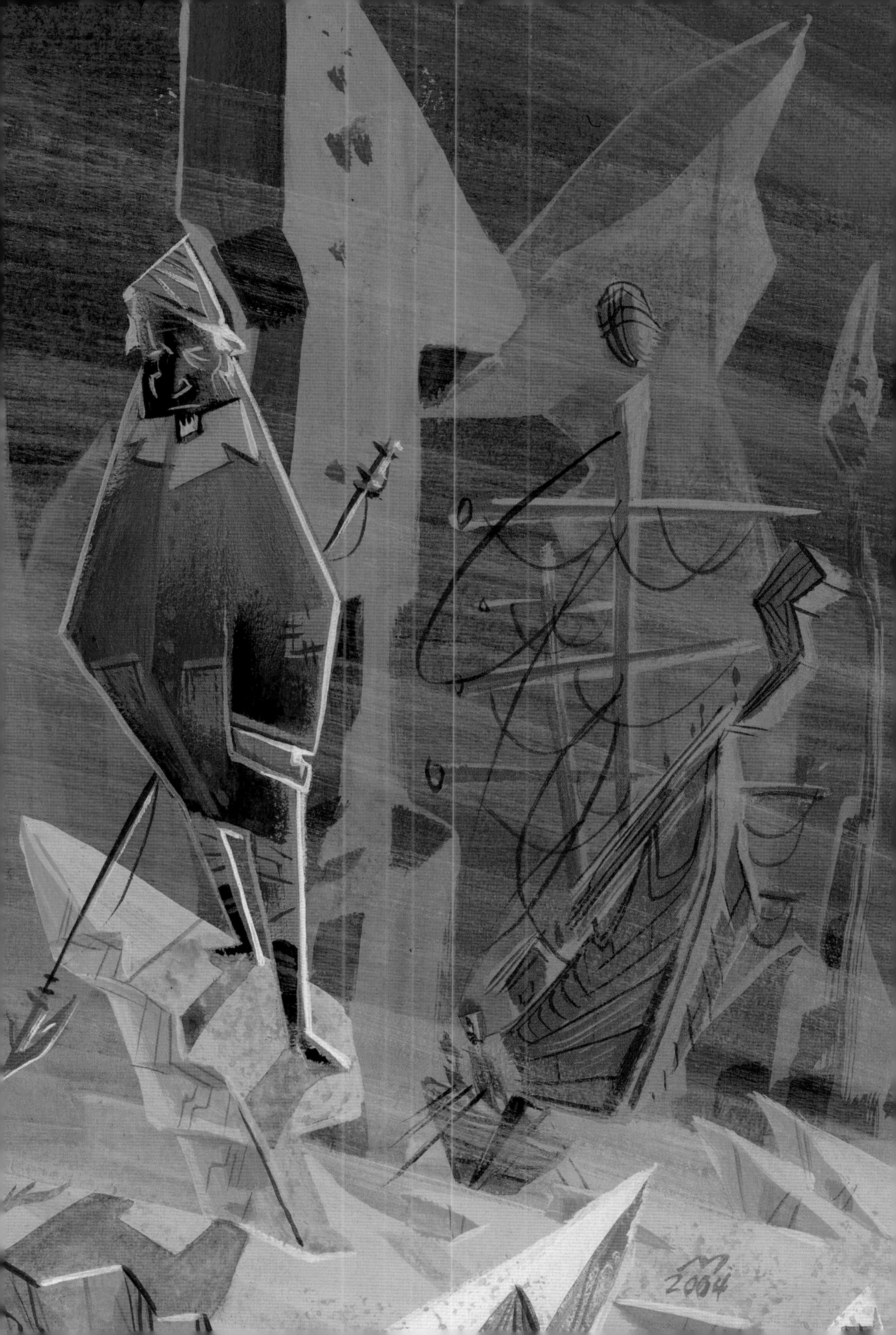

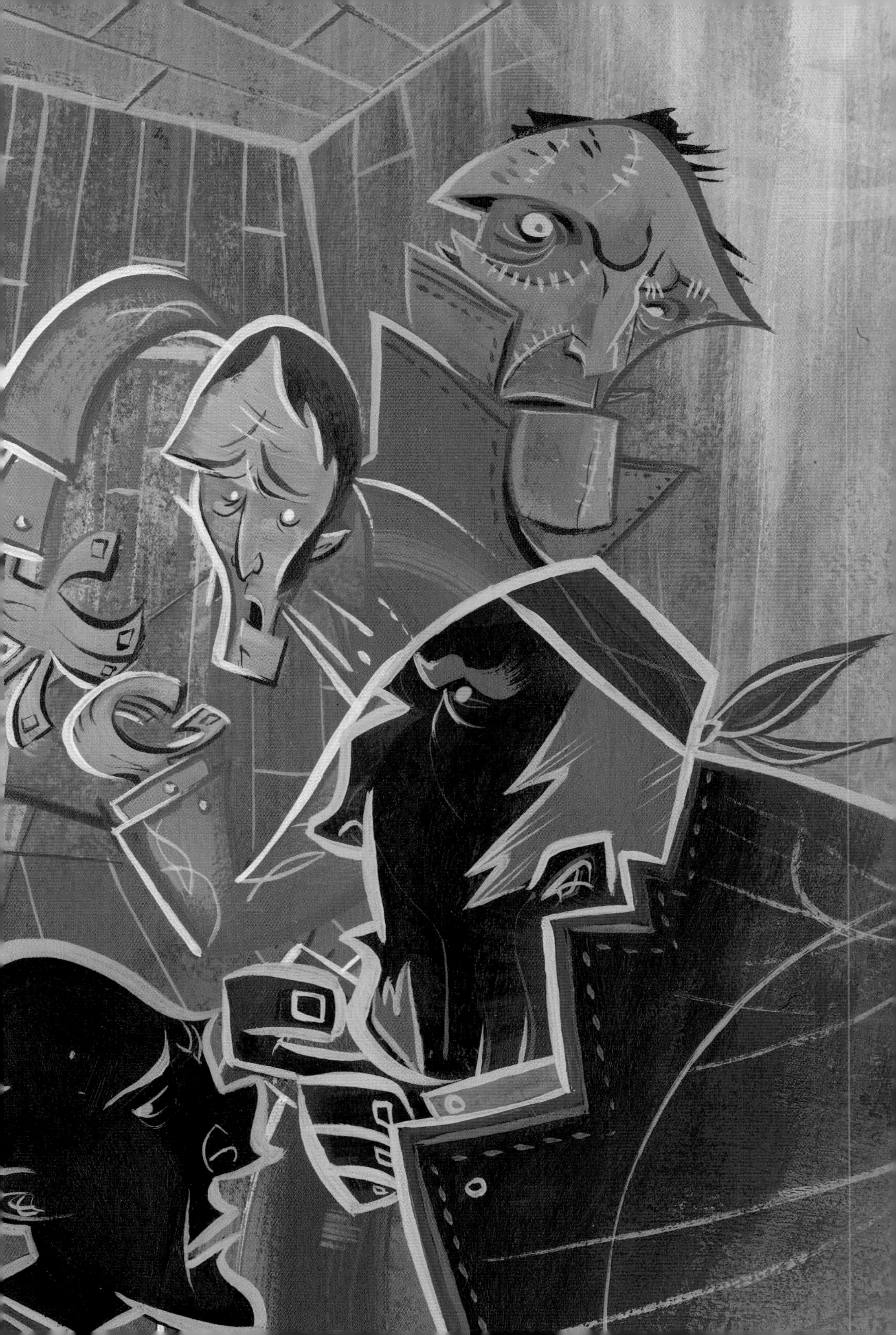

Feverish to the point of madness, Victor tells his story to Walton—the fantastic tale of the ***monster*** which Frankenstein created with his own two hands and the stolen limbs and organs of the dead!

Victor begins his story with a bit of background about his early years in Geneva and a happy childhood with his cousin Elizabeth, whom Victor would grow to love and one day marry.

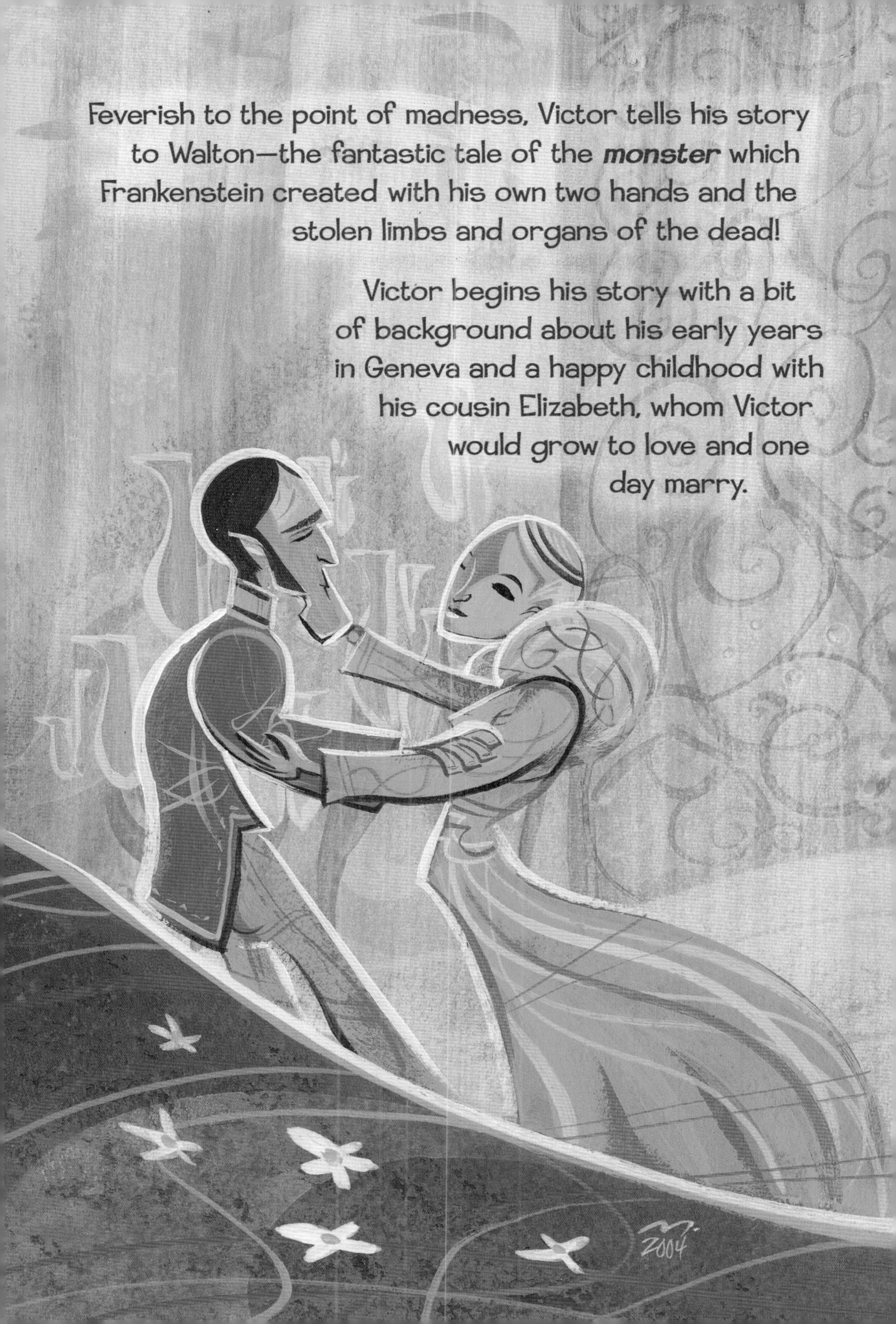

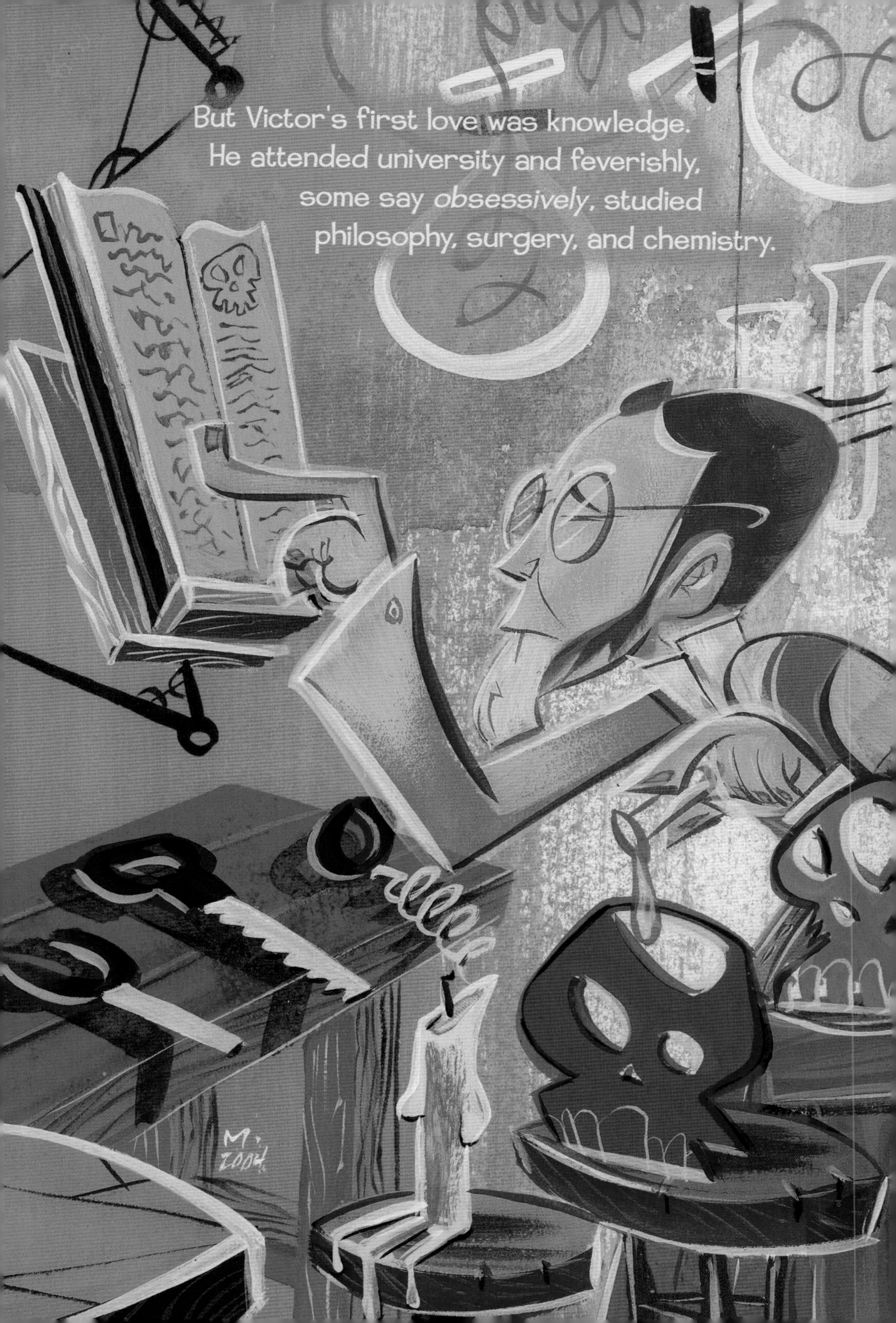
M. 2004

But Victor's first love was knowledge. He attended university and feverishly, some say *obsessively*, studied philosophy, surgery, and chemistry.

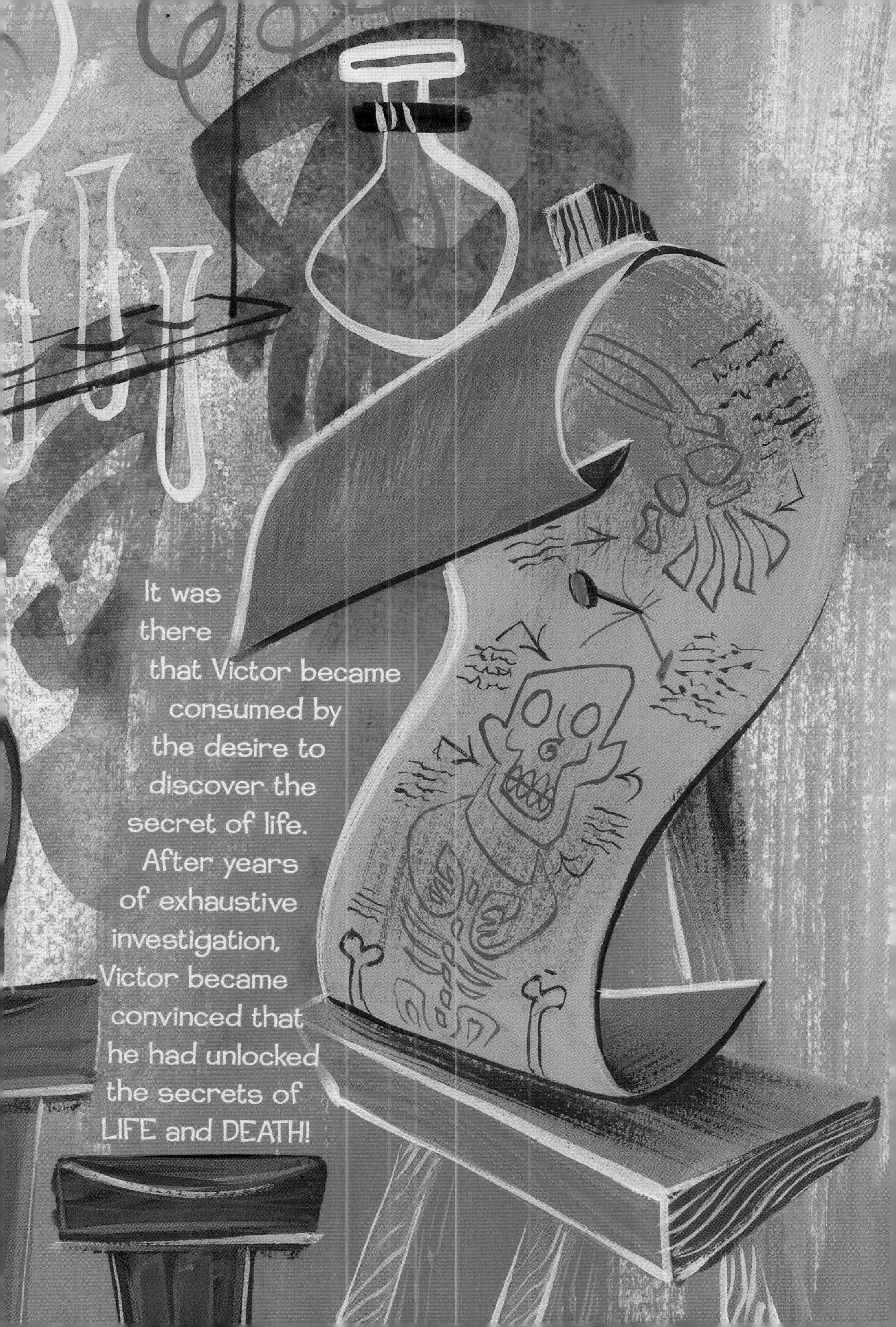

It was there that Victor became consumed by the desire to discover the secret of life. After years of exhaustive investigation, Victor became convinced that he had unlocked the secrets of LIFE and DEATH!

Victor breathlessly created a creature out of body parts. He worked around the clock, never stopping to rest. He sewed flesh to flesh, reattached intricate nerves and cauterized arteries. Organ by organ, he built a man that never was out of pieces of people who once were.

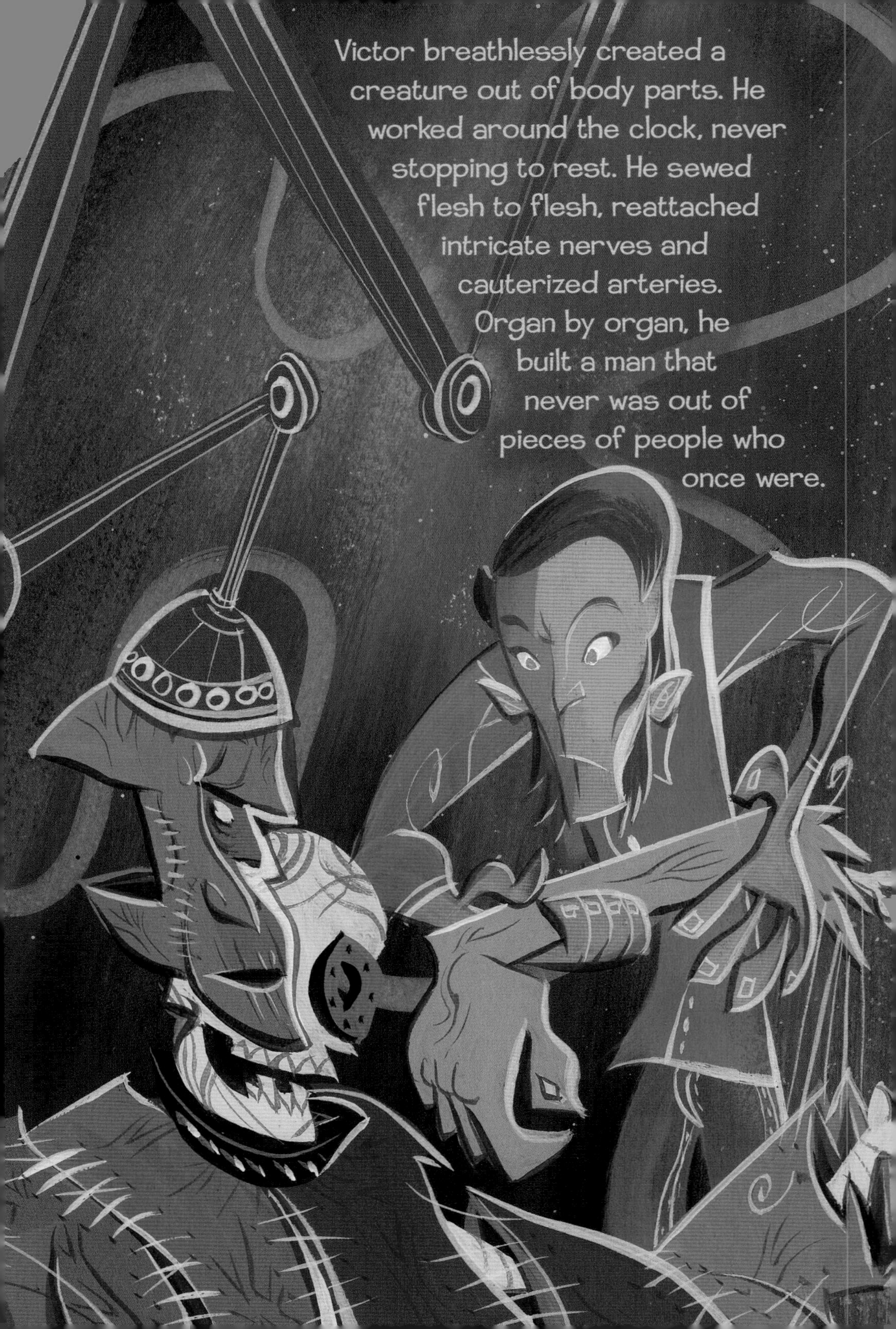

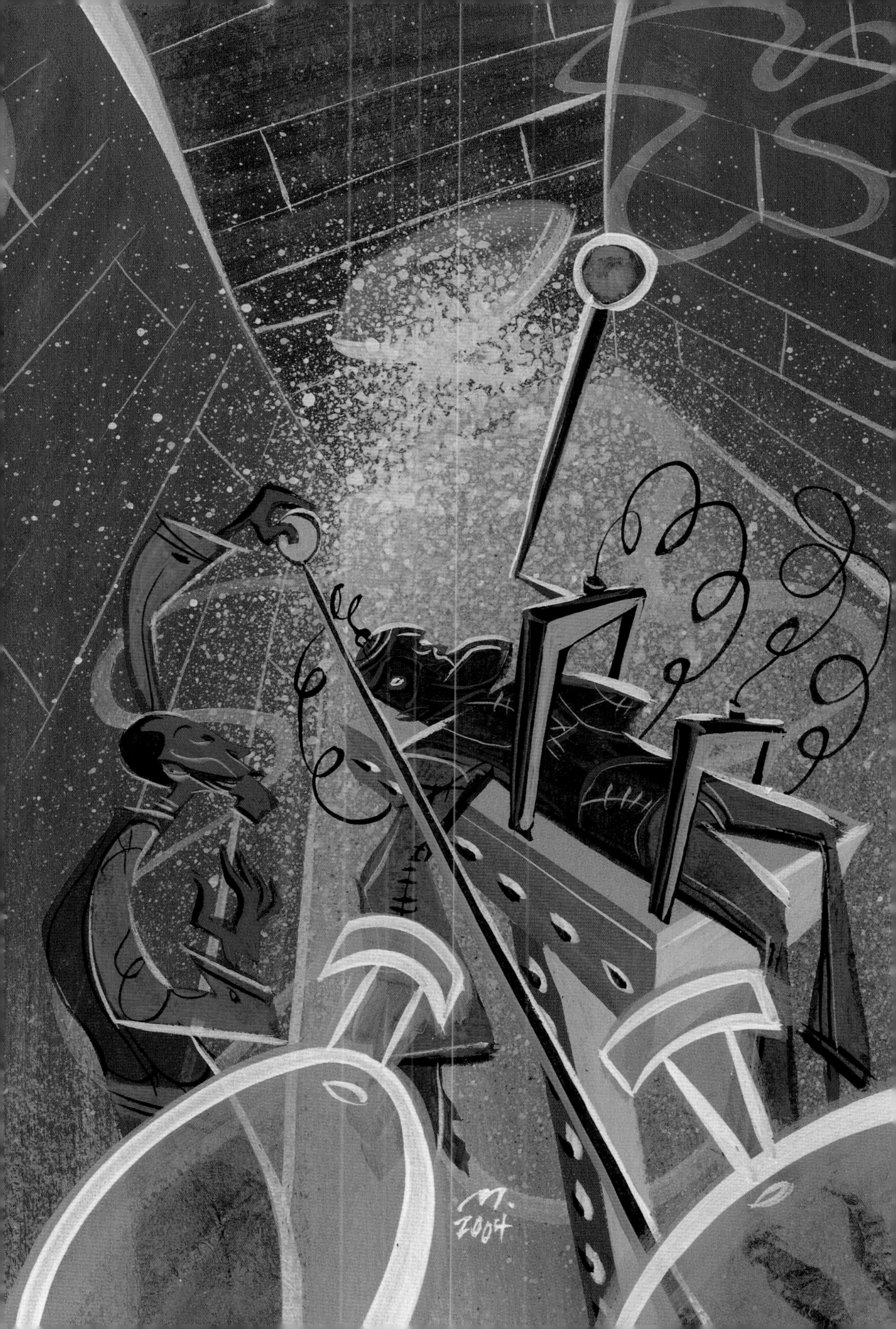
M.
2004

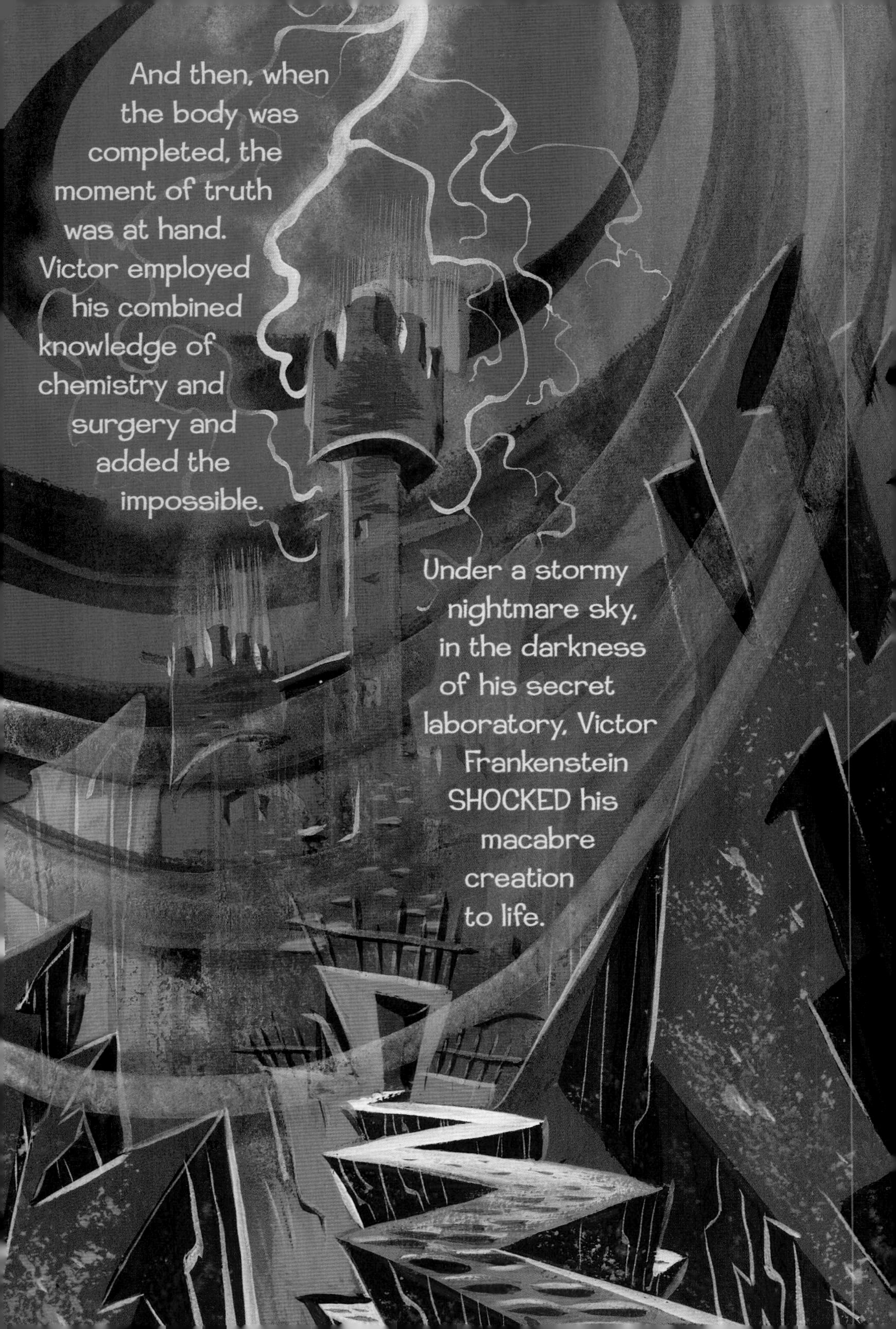
And then, when the body was completed, the moment of truth was at hand. Victor employed his combined knowledge of chemistry and surgery and added the impossible.
Under a stormy nightmare sky, in the darkness of his secret laboratory, Victor Frankenstein SHOCKED his macabre creation to life.

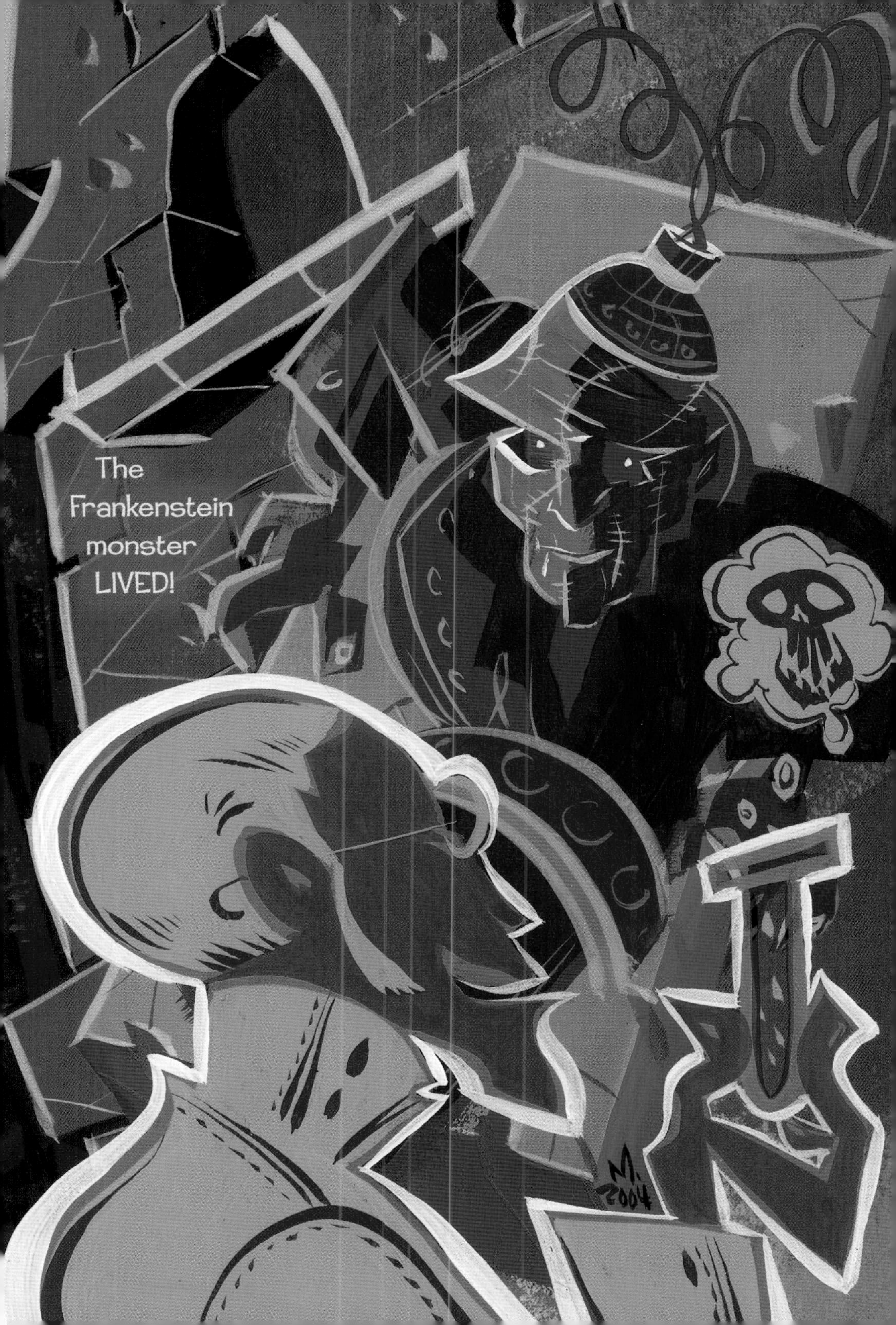
The Frankenstein monster LIVED!
M. 2004

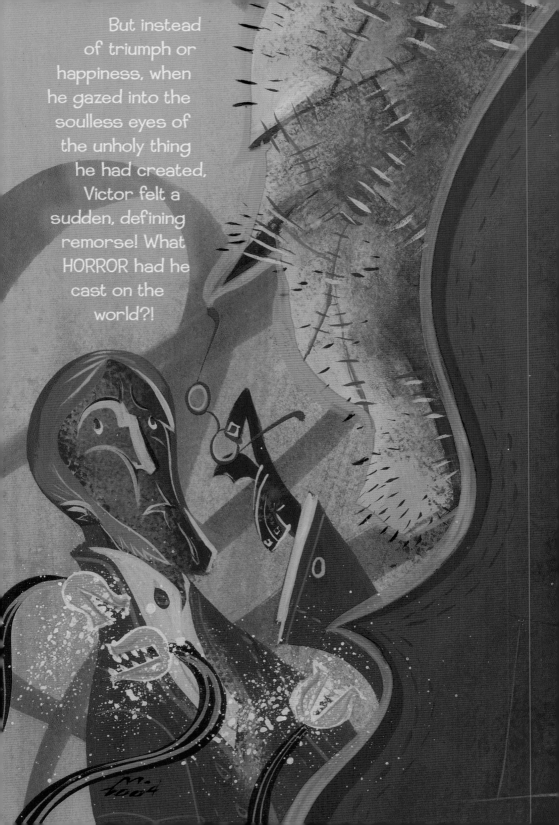

But instead of triumph or happiness, when he gazed into the soulless eyes of the unholy thing he had created, Victor felt a sudden, defining remorse! What HORROR had he cast on the world?!

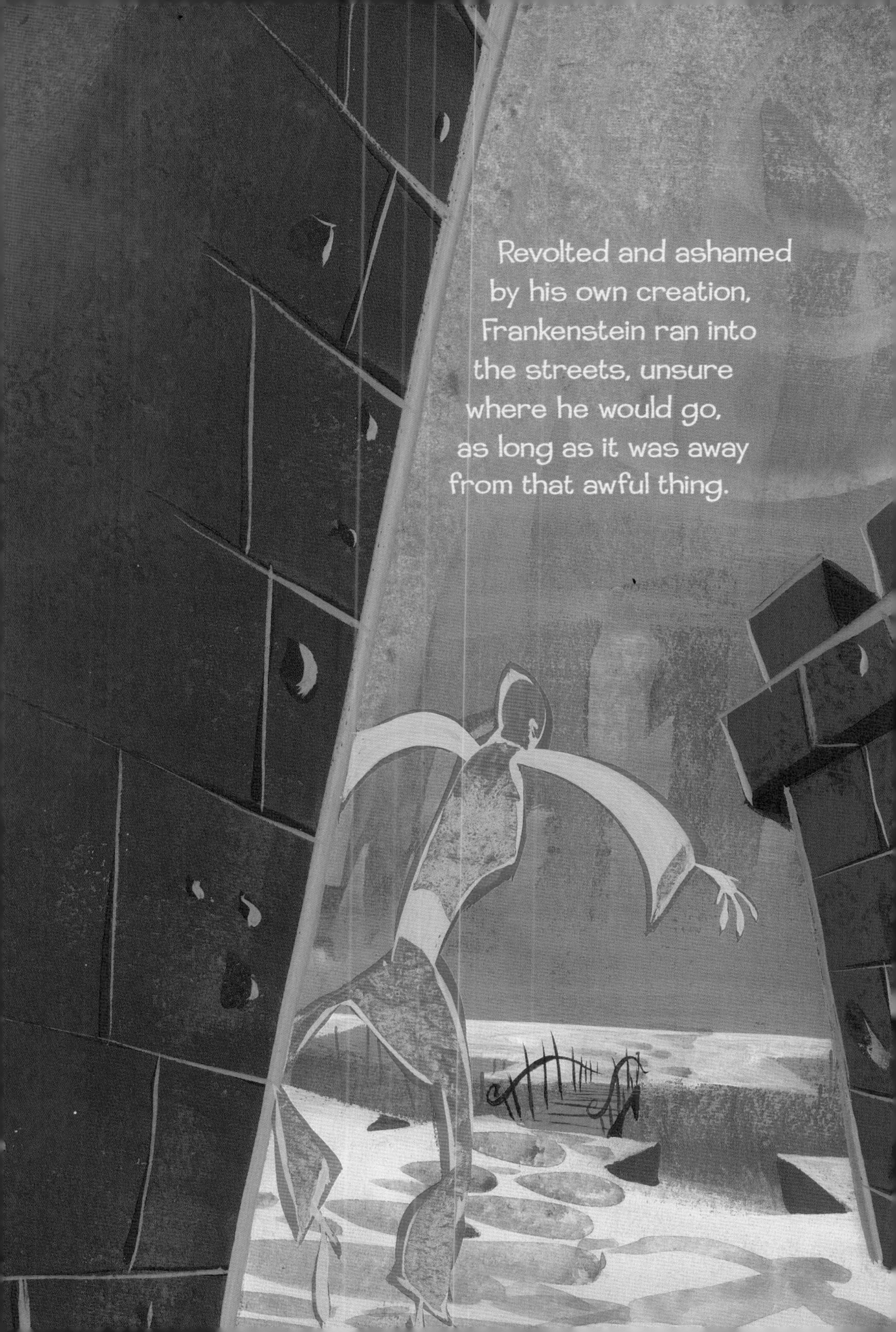

Revolted and ashamed by his own creation, Frankenstein ran into the streets, unsure where he would go, as long as it was away from that awful thing.

Weak and unable to live with the abomination he had wrought, Victor fell into months of fever and illness, never forgetting the CREATURE still lived somewhere out there and he was to blame.

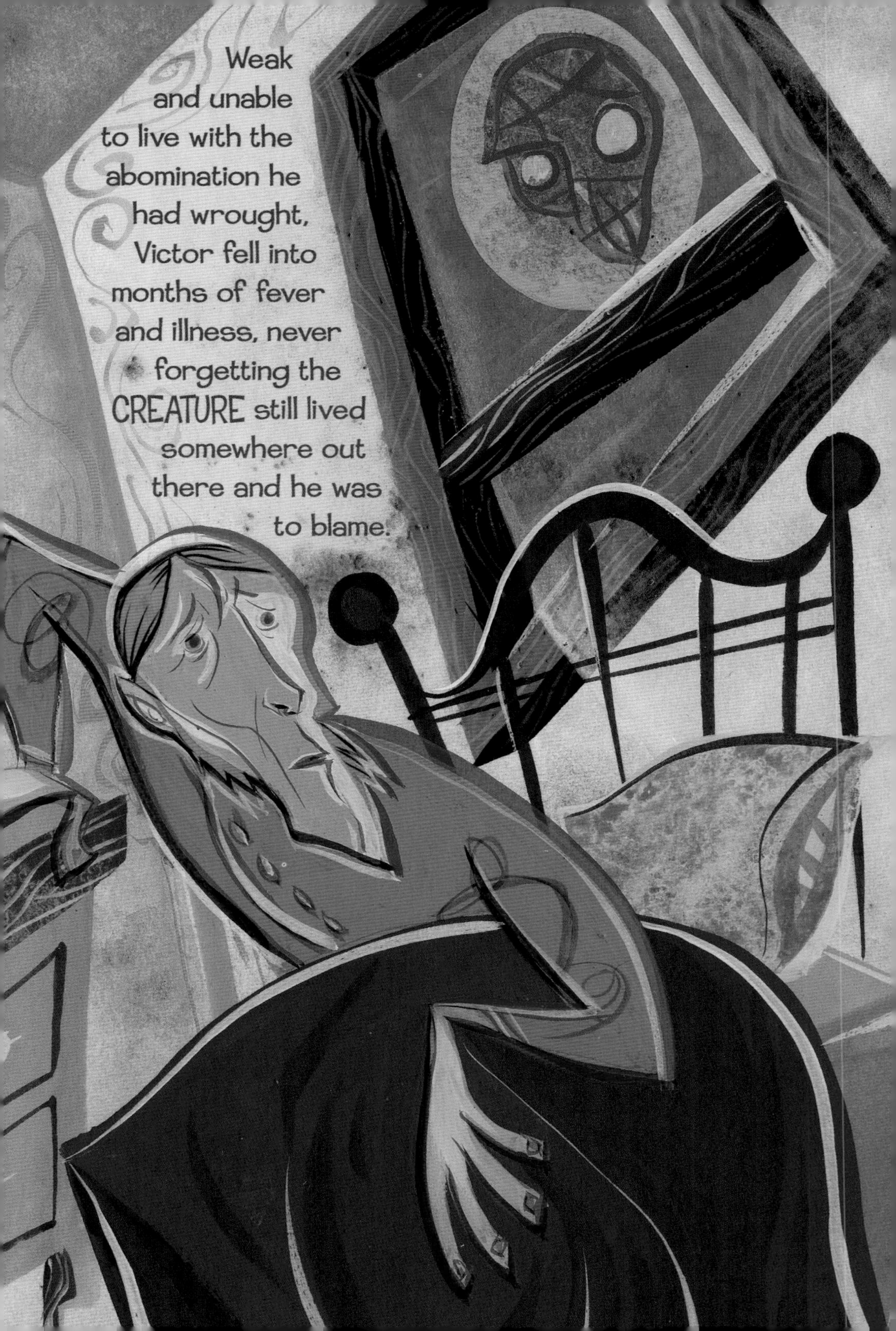

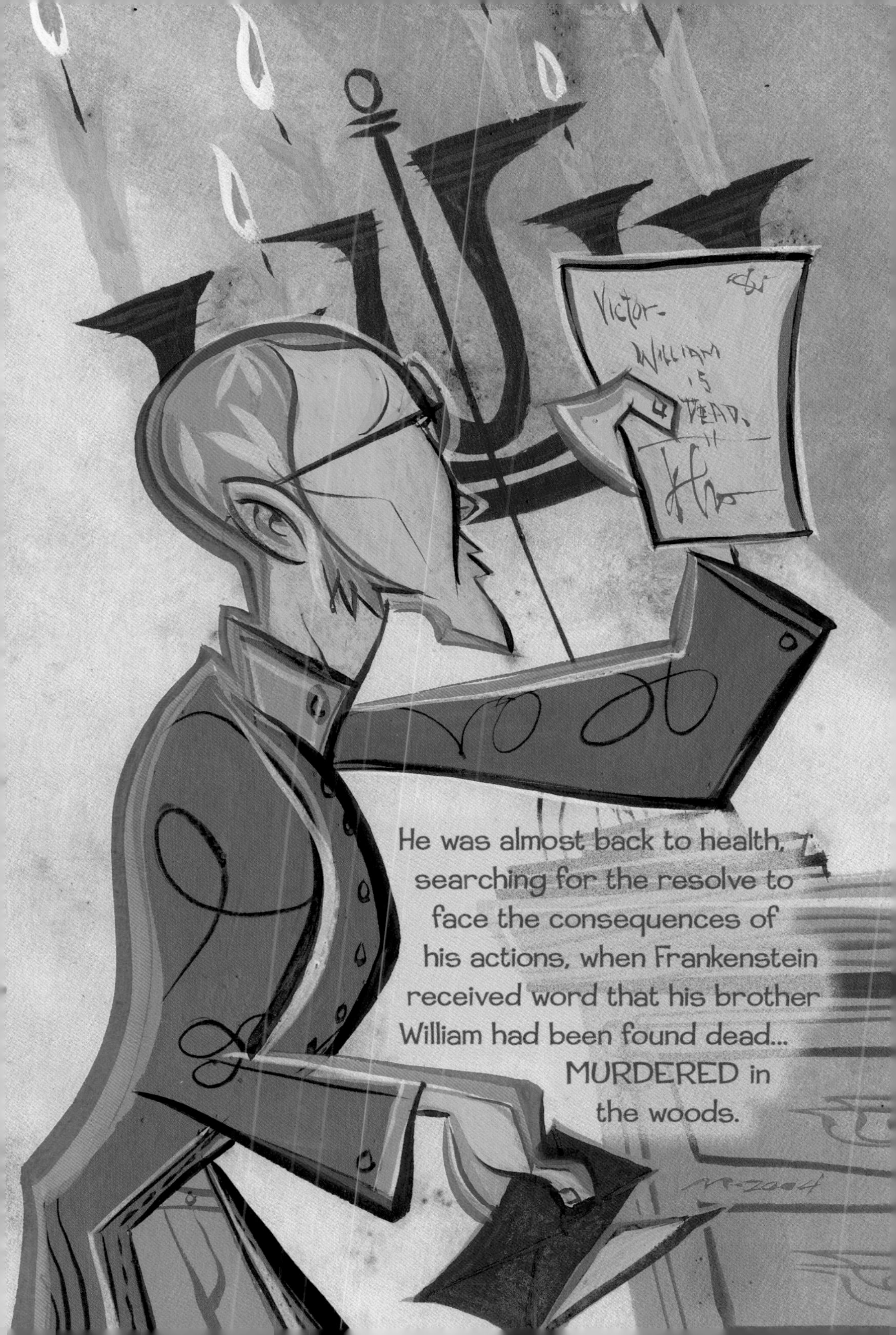
Victor-
William
is
DEAD.

He was almost back to health, searching for the resolve to face the consequences of his actions, when Frankenstein received word that his brother William had been found dead... MURDERED in the woods.

Grief-stricken and suspecting the monster of committing the crime, Victor hurried home and attended the funeral.

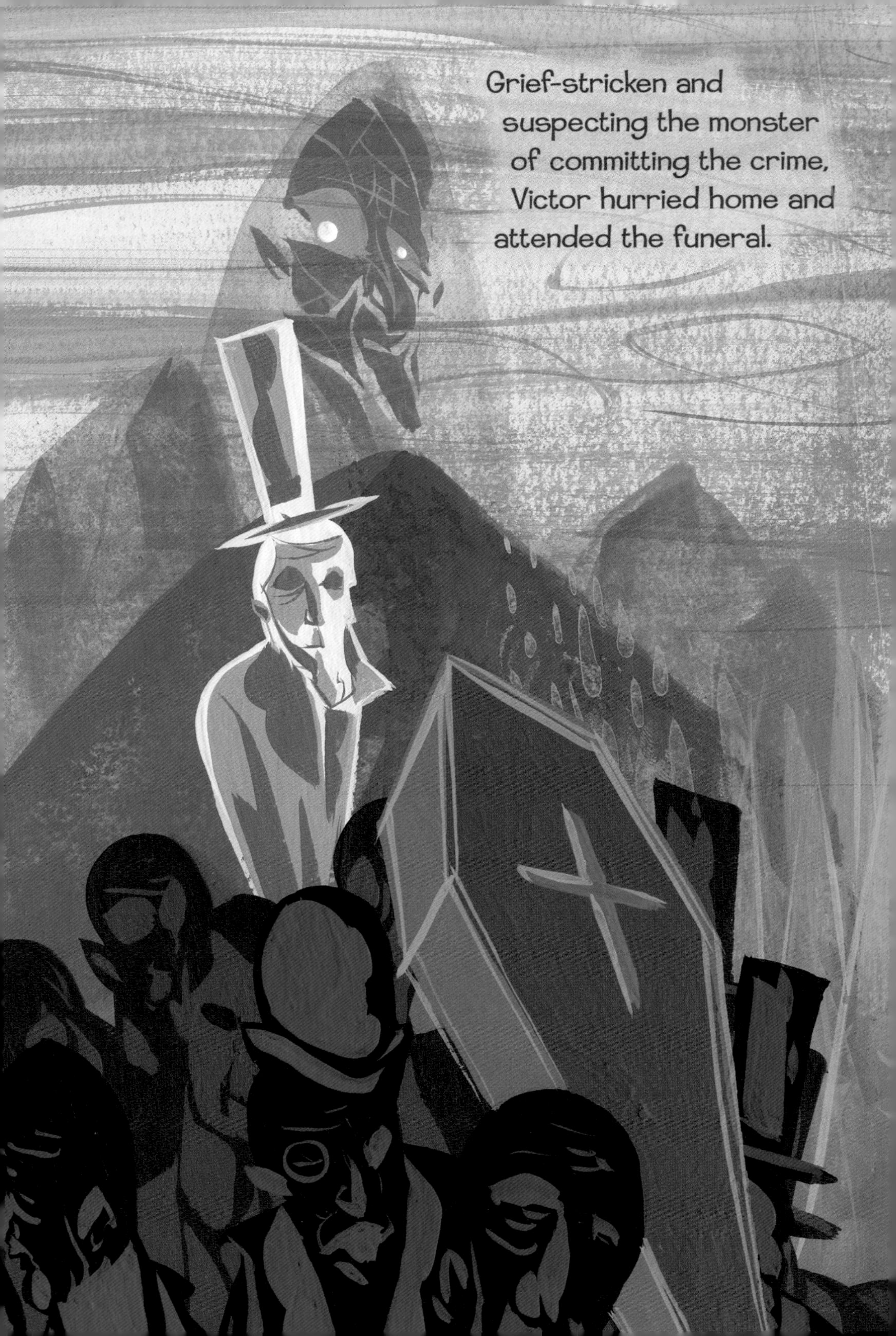

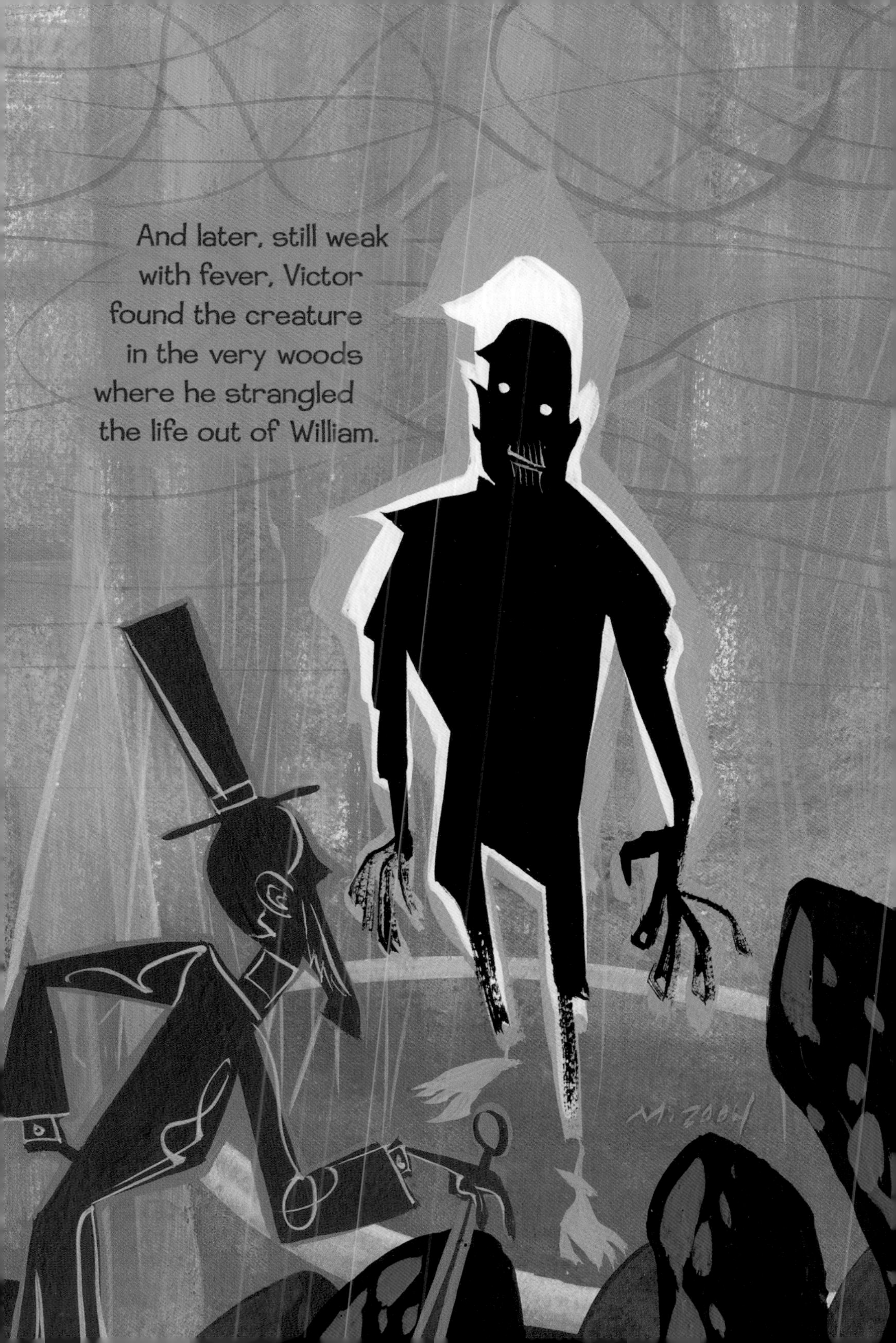
And later, still weak
with fever, Victor
found the creature
in the very woods
where he strangled
the life out of William.

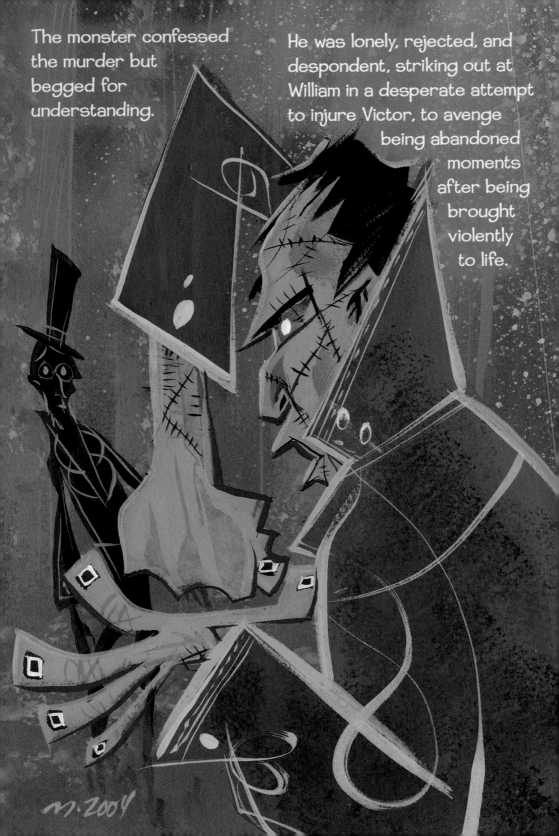

The monster confessed the murder but begged for understanding.

He was lonely, rejected, and despondent, striking out at William in a desperate attempt to injure Victor, to avenge being abandoned moments after being brought violently to life.

m·2004

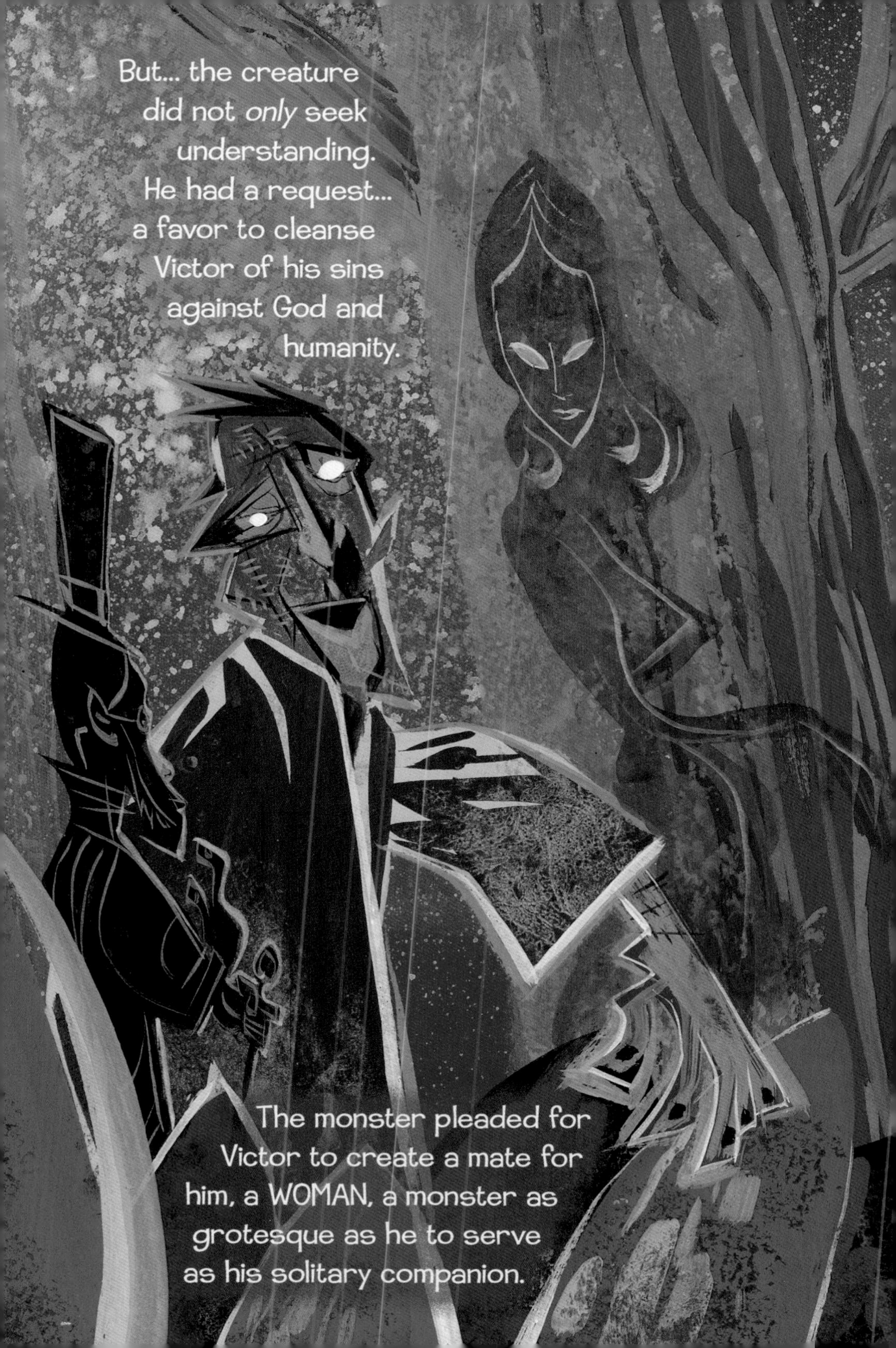
But... the creature did not *only* seek understanding. He had a request... a favor to cleanse Victor of his sins against God and humanity.
The monster pleaded for Victor to create a mate for him, a WOMAN, a monster as grotesque as he to serve as his solitary companion.

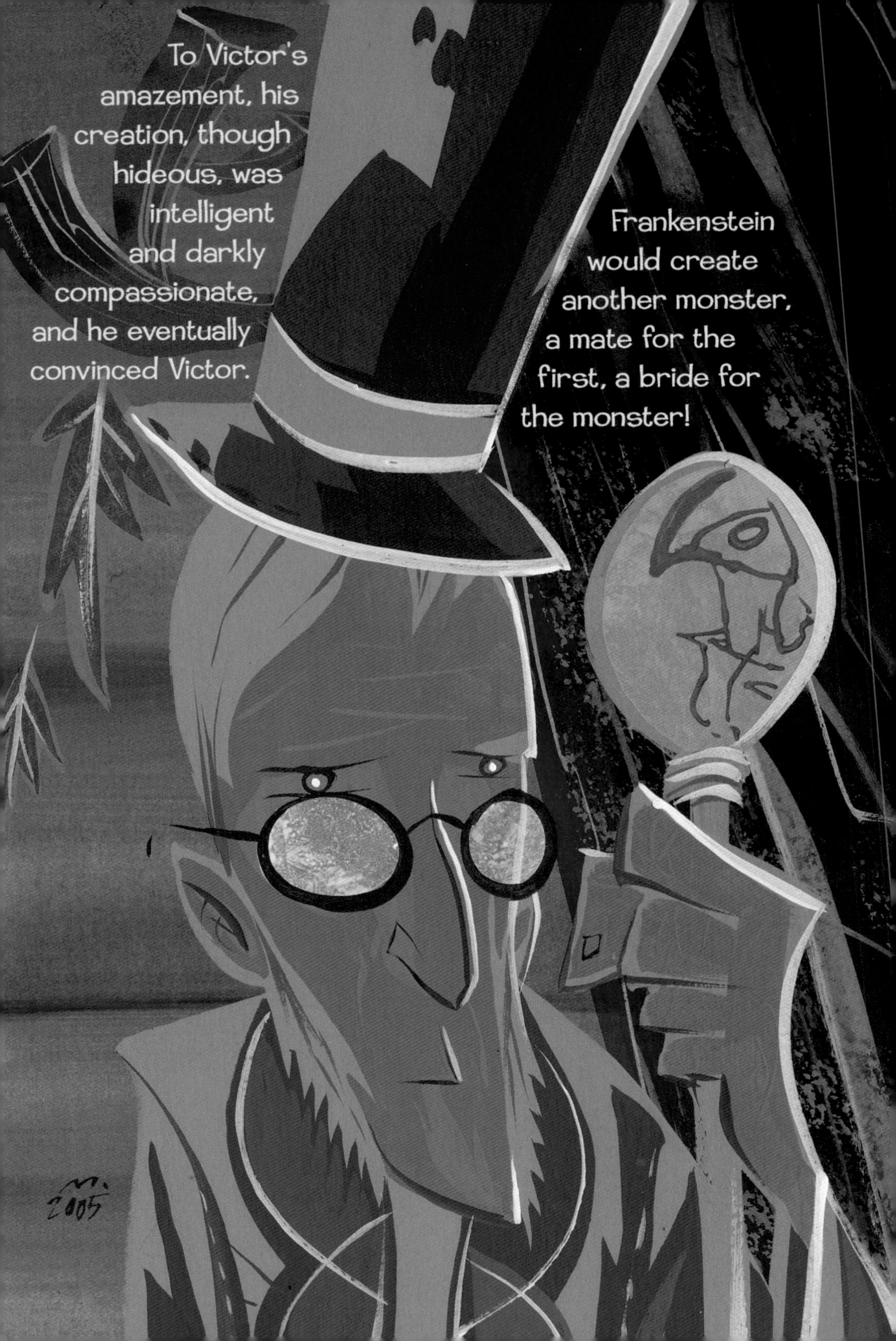
To Victor's amazement, his creation, though hideous, was intelligent and darkly compassionate, and he eventually convinced Victor.
Frankenstein would create another monster, a mate for the first, a bride for the monster!

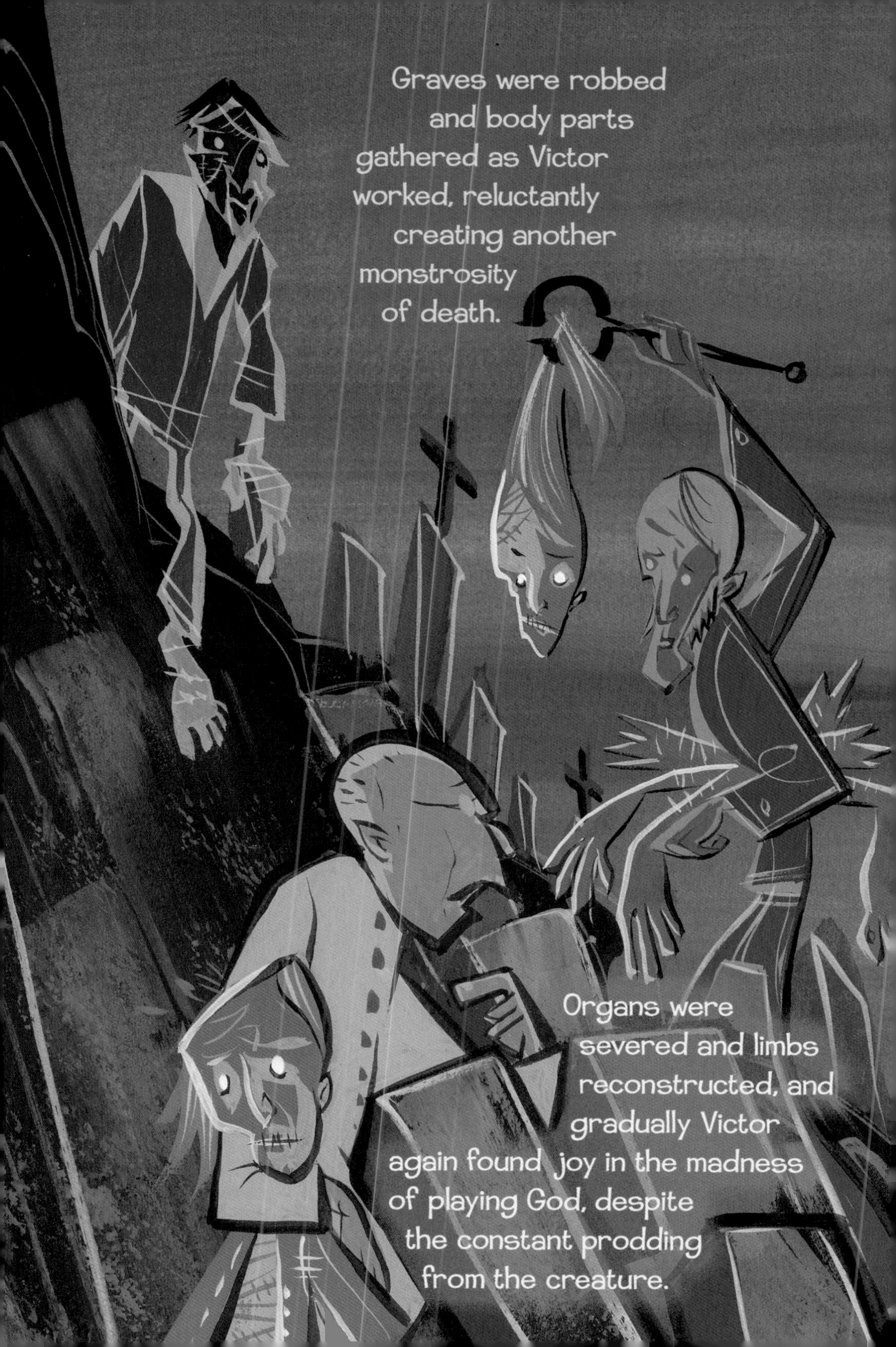

Graves were robbed and body parts gathered as Victor worked, reluctantly creating another monstrosity of death.

Organs were severed and limbs reconstructed, and gradually Victor again found joy in the madness of playing God, despite the constant prodding from the creature.

He would not leave him to work, always prodding, always peering in as he worked and waking him when he attempted to rest. That was the one thing Victor could not return to his creation. It never slept, and so, neither would he.

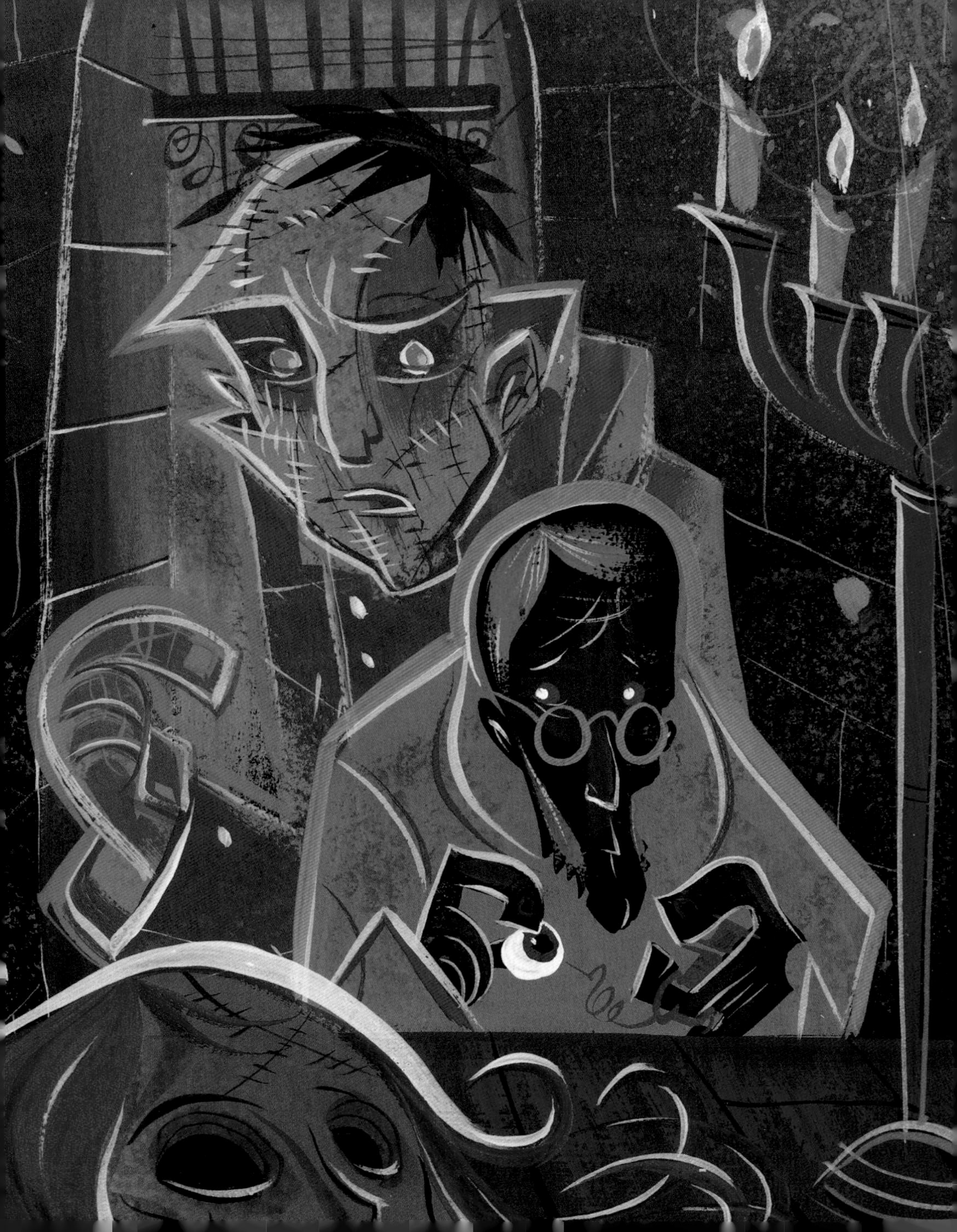

Once alive, he saw sadness in the new monster's eyes and he knew instantly he could not condemn her to a life trapped in that murdering monster's arms!

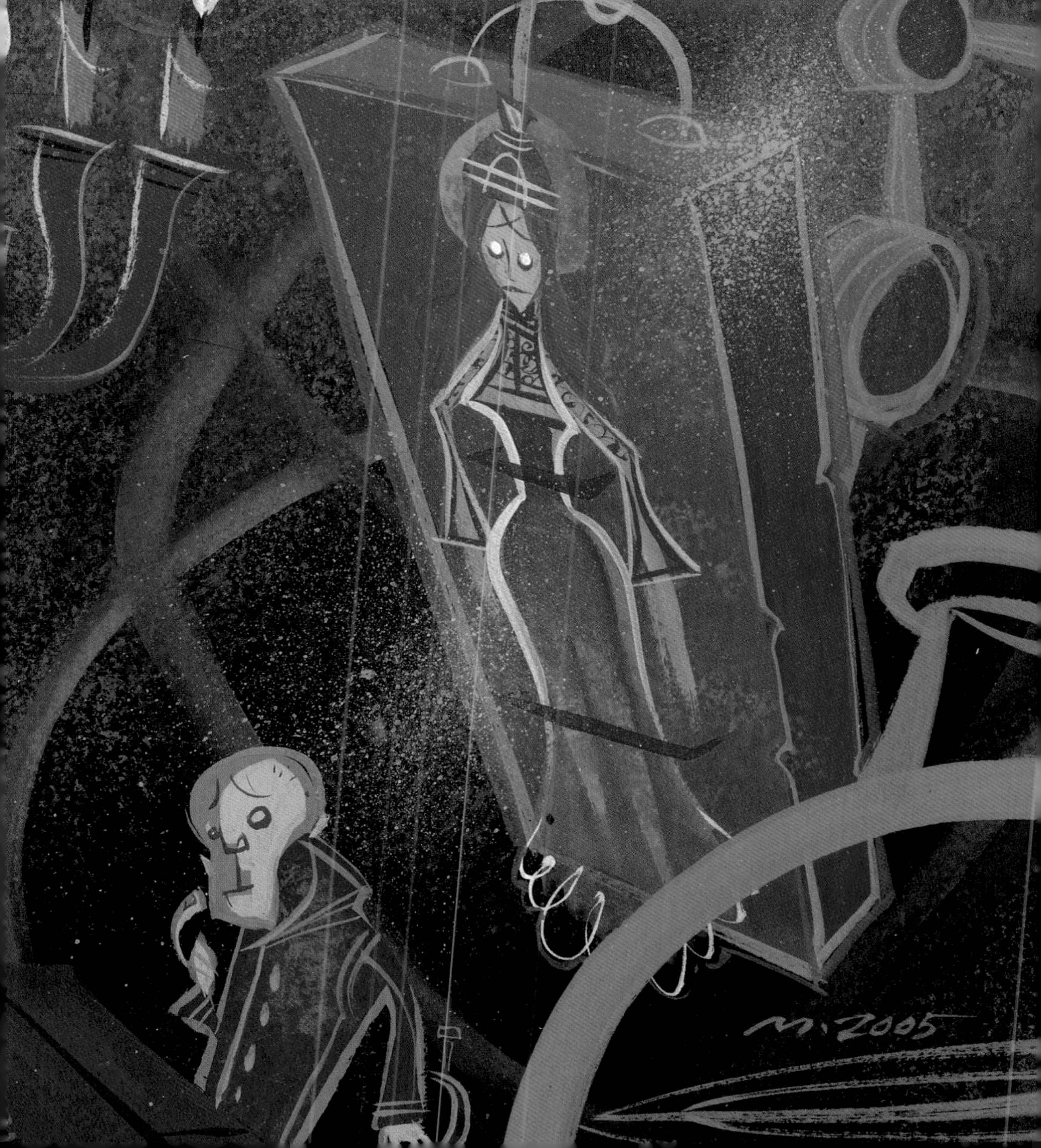

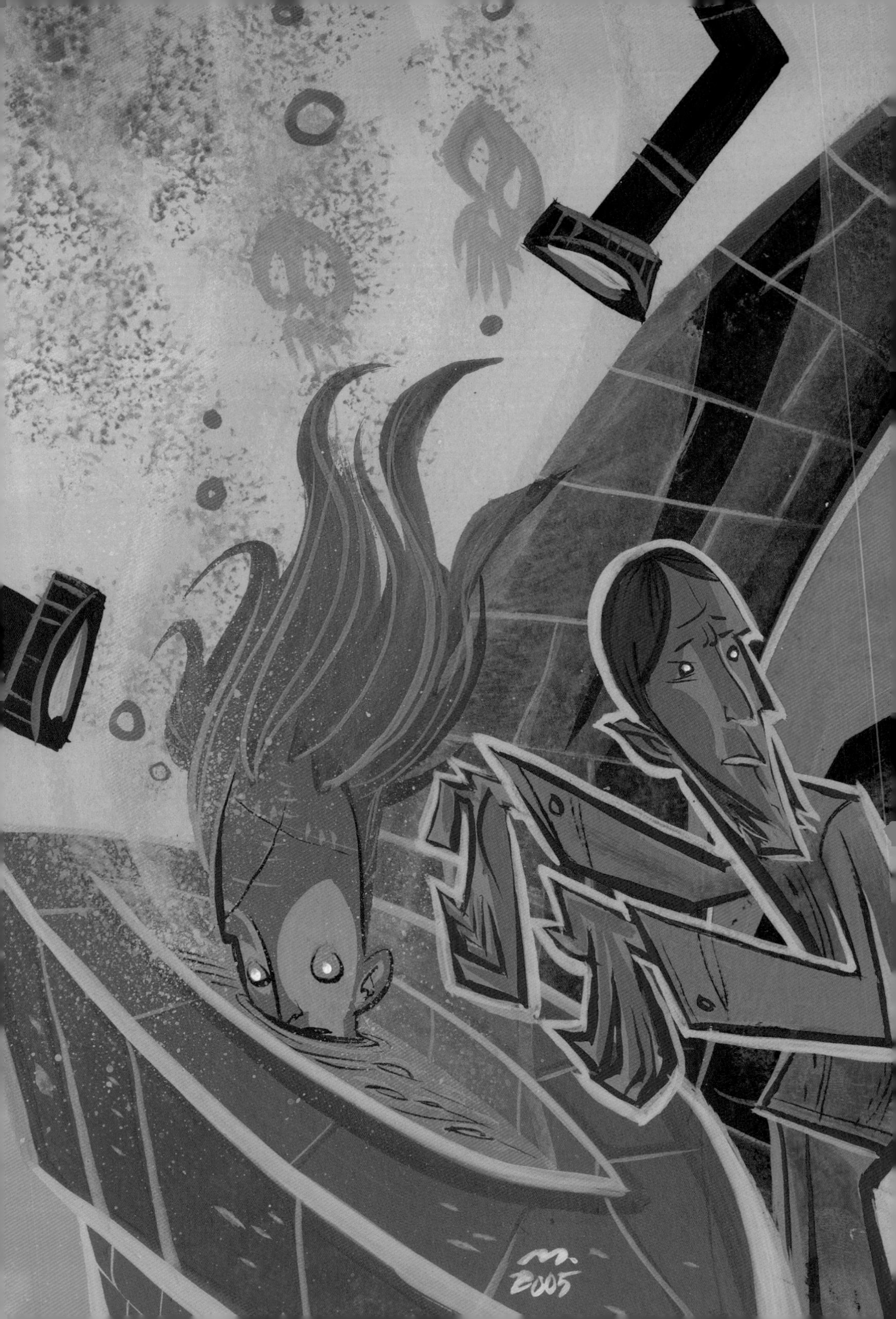
m.
2005

Horrified by the sudden realization of what he had done, Victor destroyed his new creation, immersing her *still-living* form into a tub of ACID right before the monster's eyes!

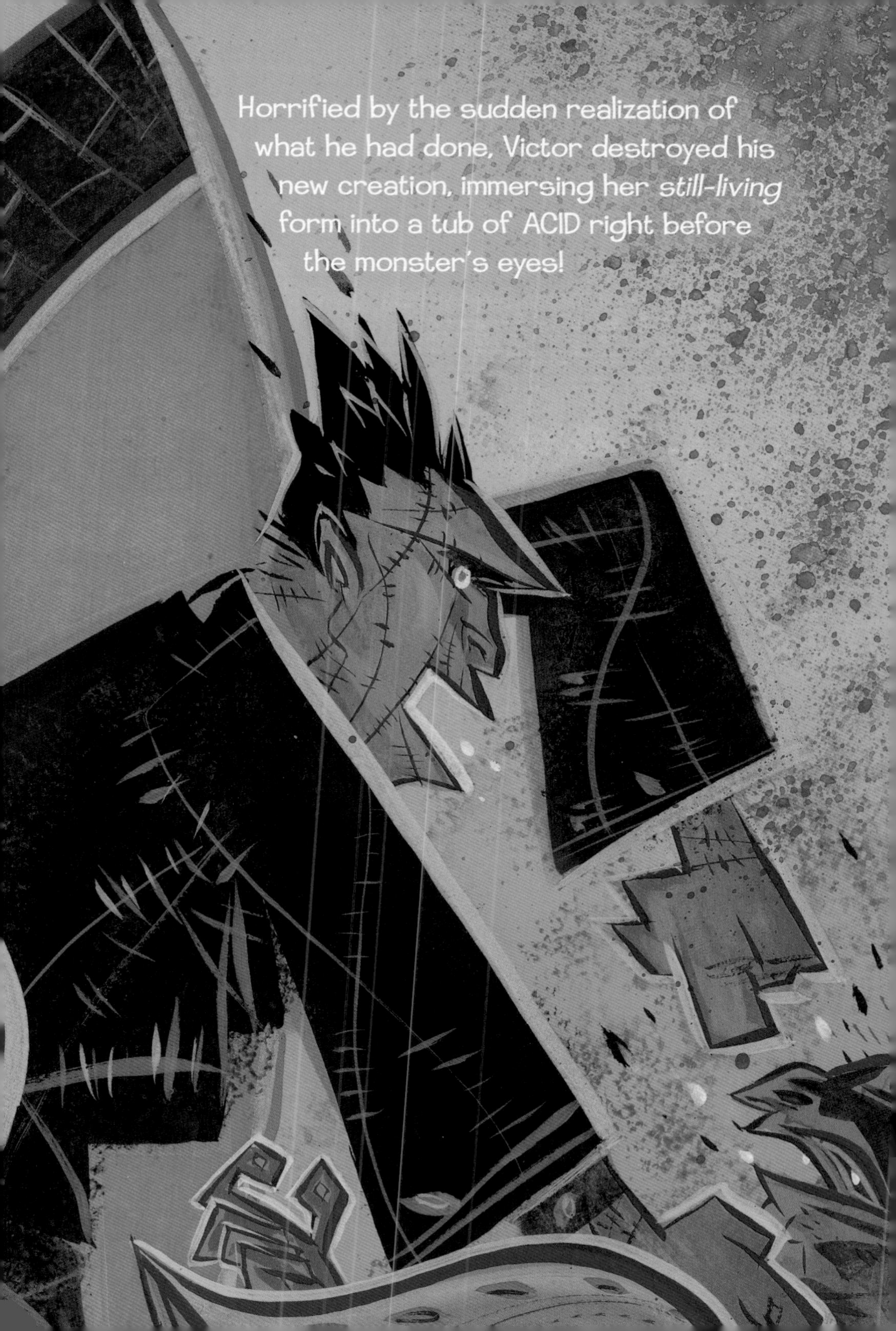

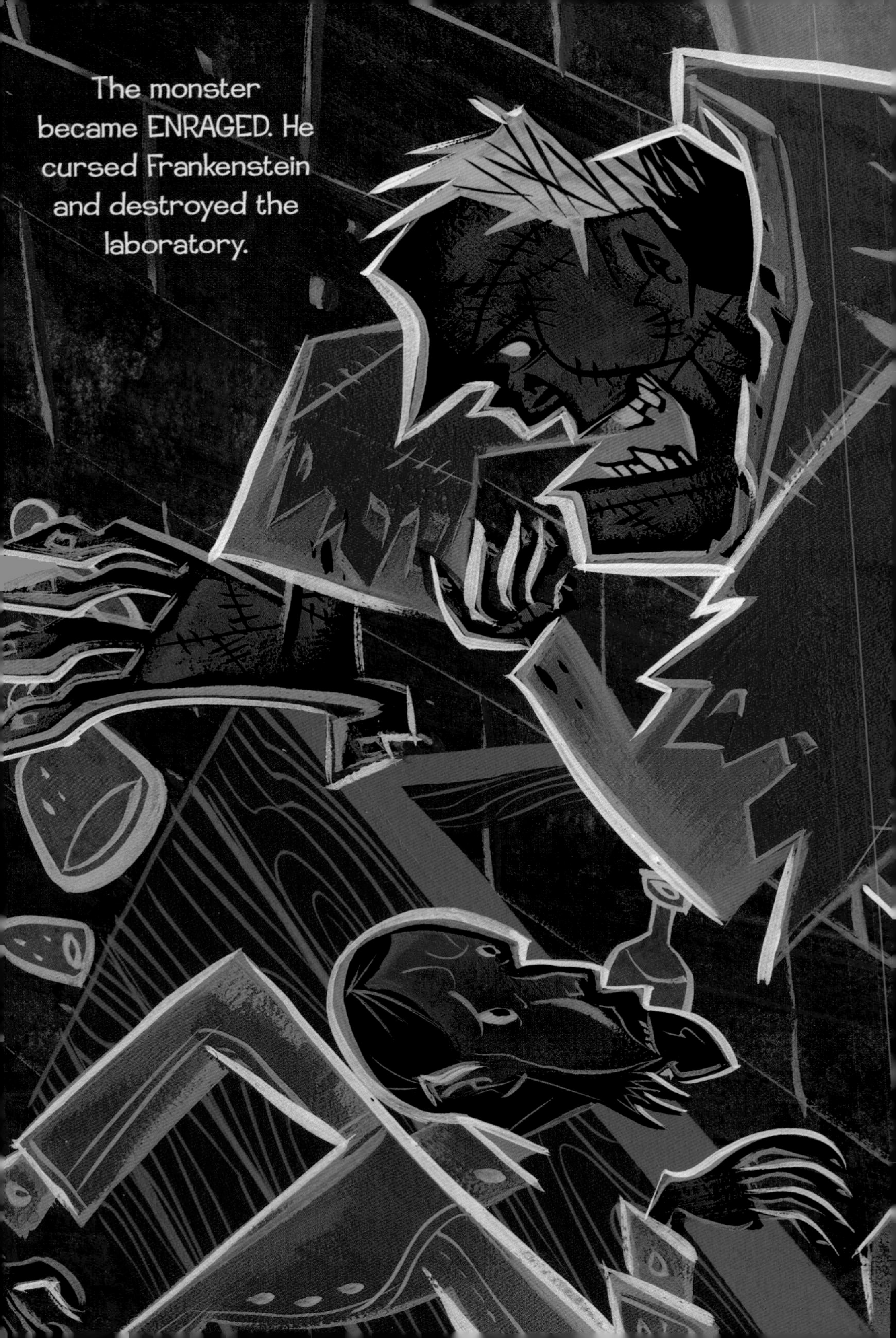
The monster became ENRAGED. He cursed Frankenstein and destroyed the laboratory.

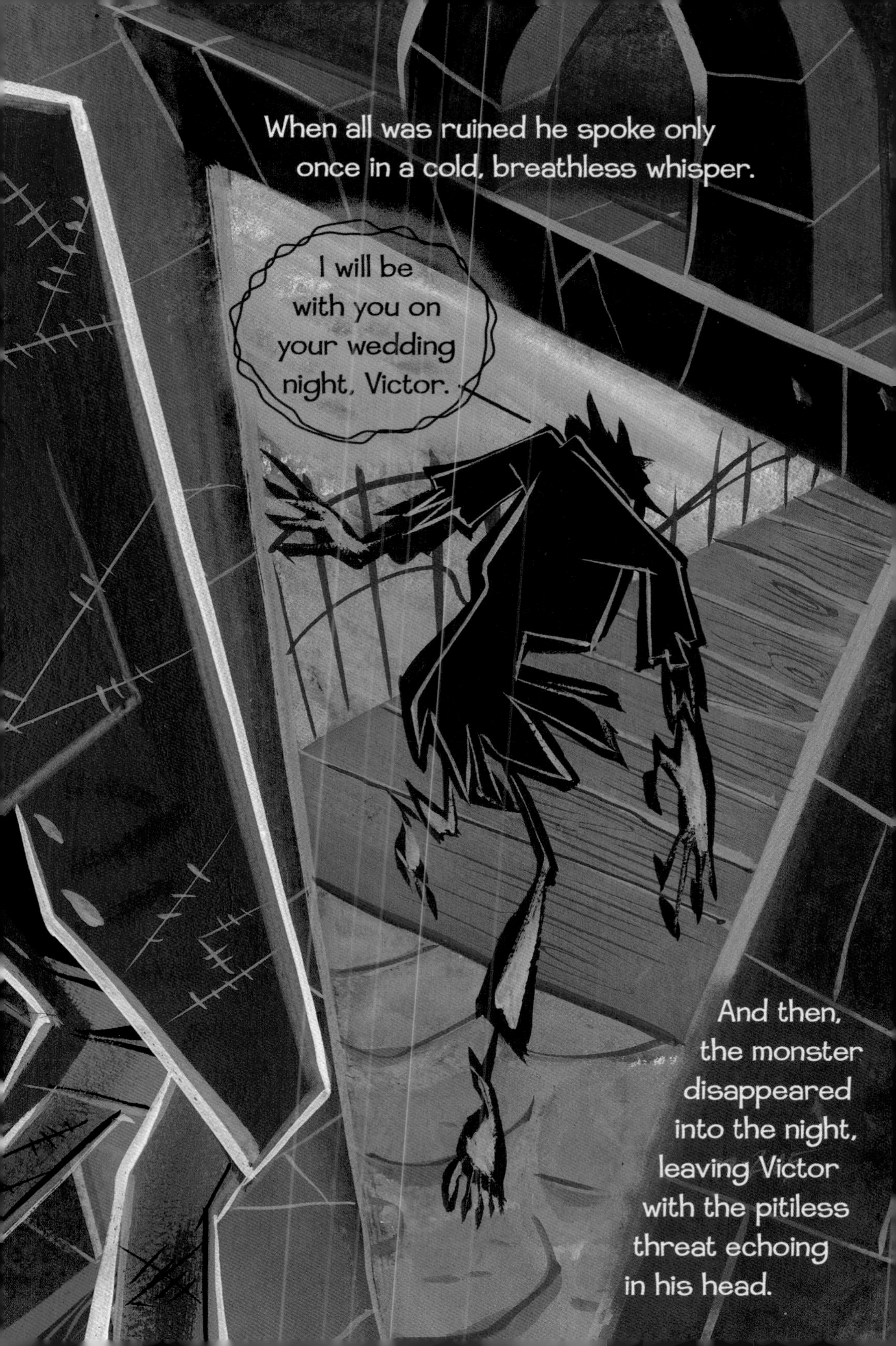
When all was ruined he spoke only once in a cold, breathless whisper.
I will be with you on your wedding night, Victor.
And then, the monster disappeared into the night, leaving Victor with the pitiless threat echoing in his head.

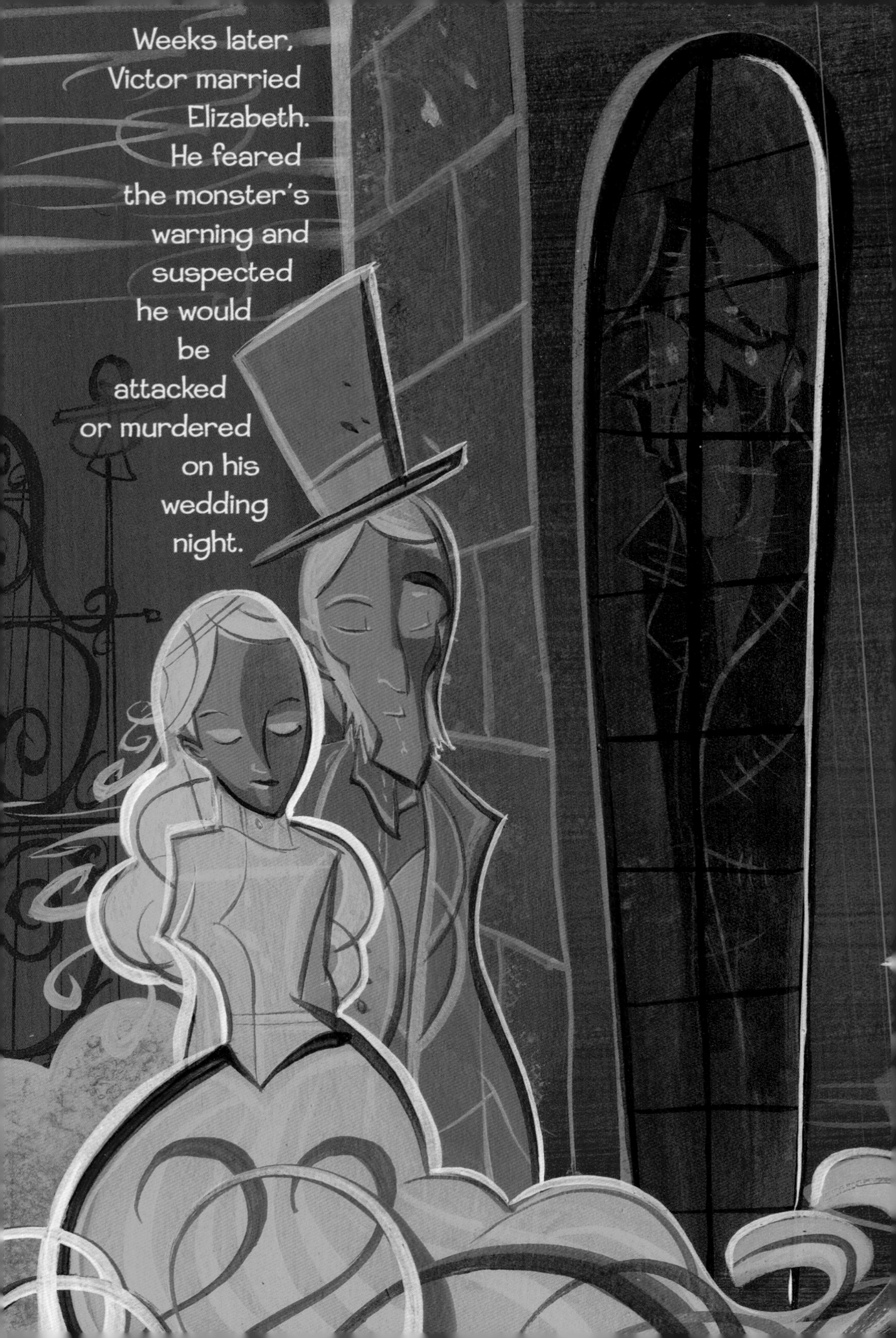
Weeks later, Victor married Elizabeth. He feared the monster's warning and suspected he would be attacked or murdered on his wedding night.

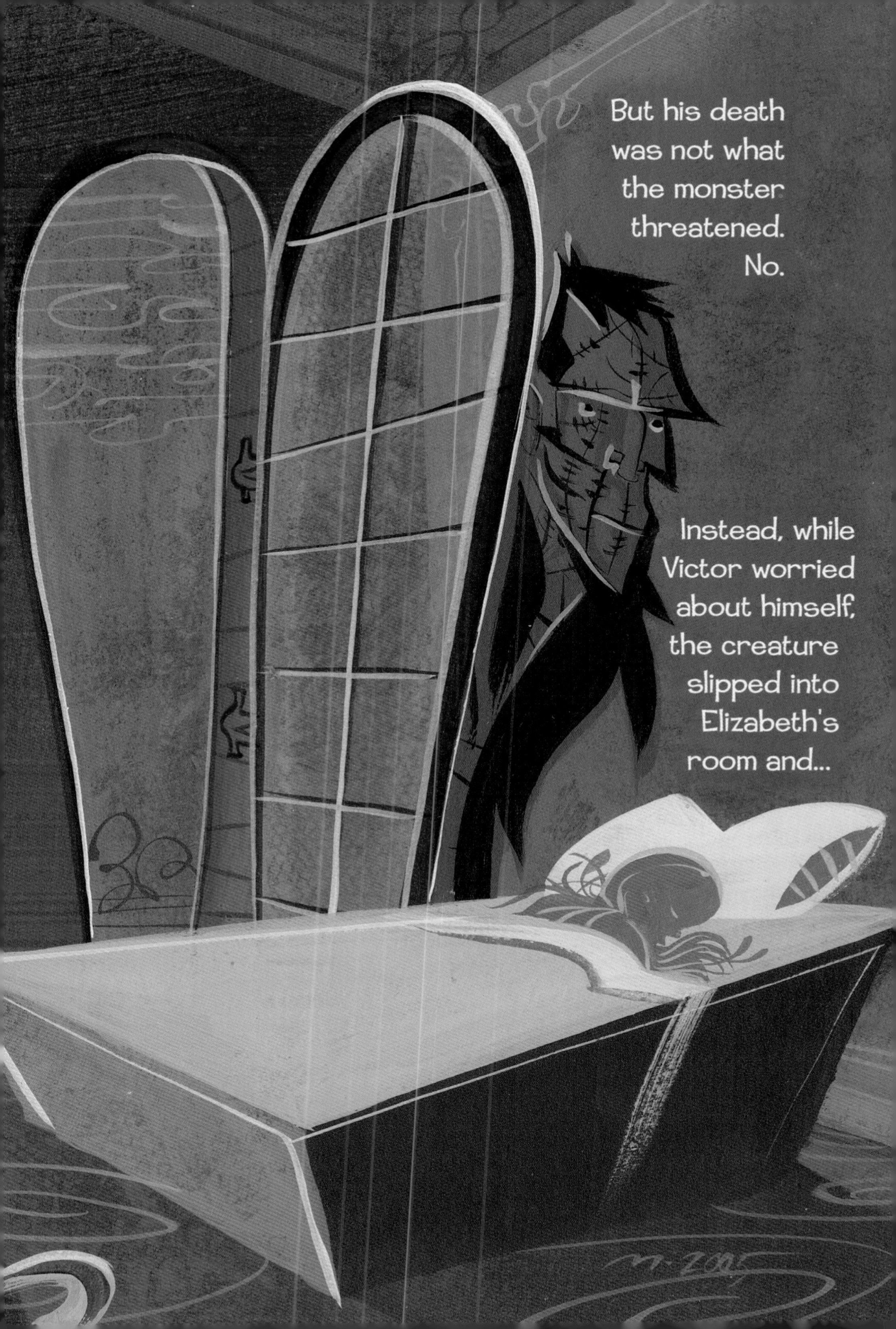

But his death was not what the monster threatened. No.

Instead, while Victor worried about himself, the creature slipped into Elizabeth's room and...

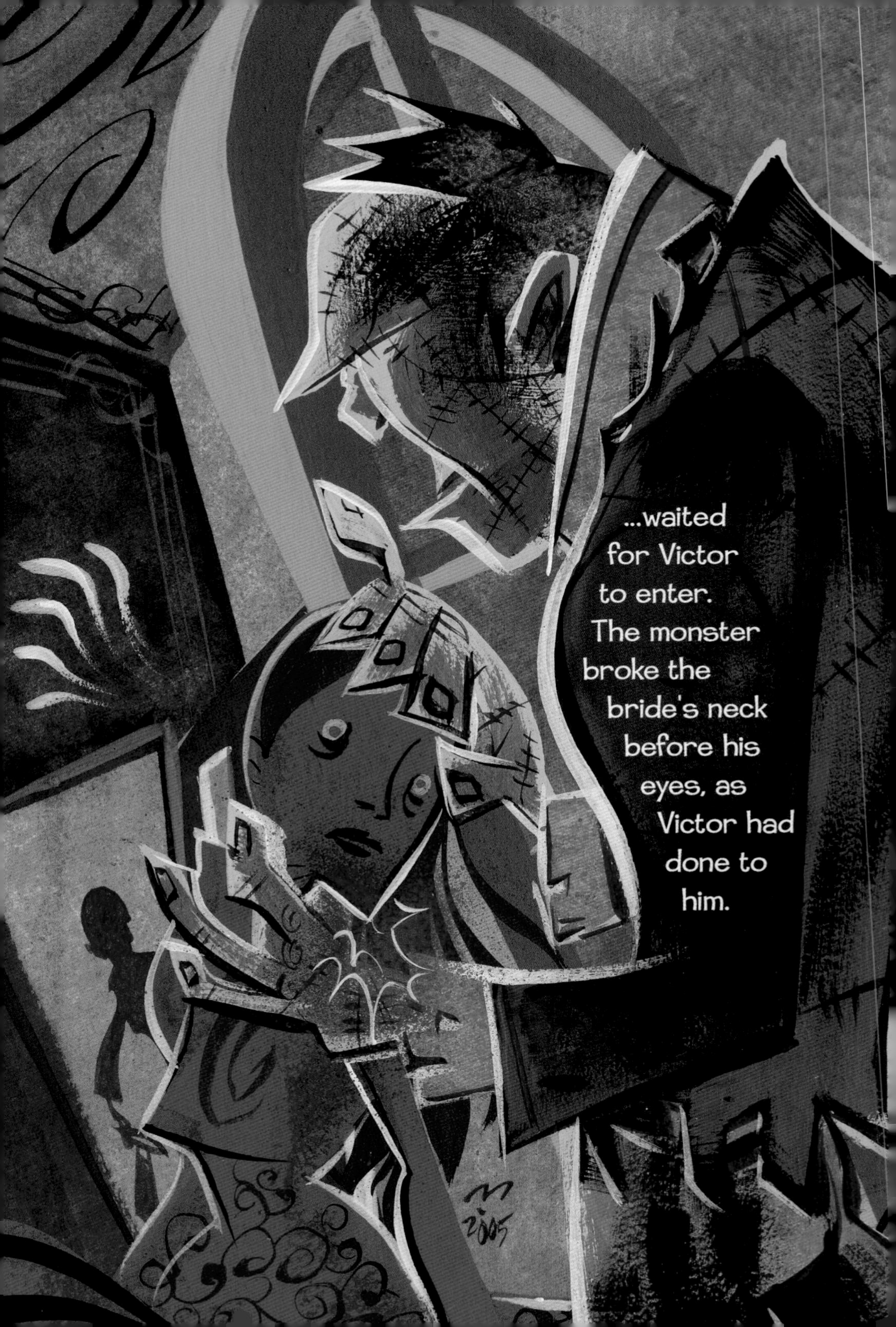
...waited for Victor to enter. The monster broke the bride's neck before his eyes, as Victor had done to him.

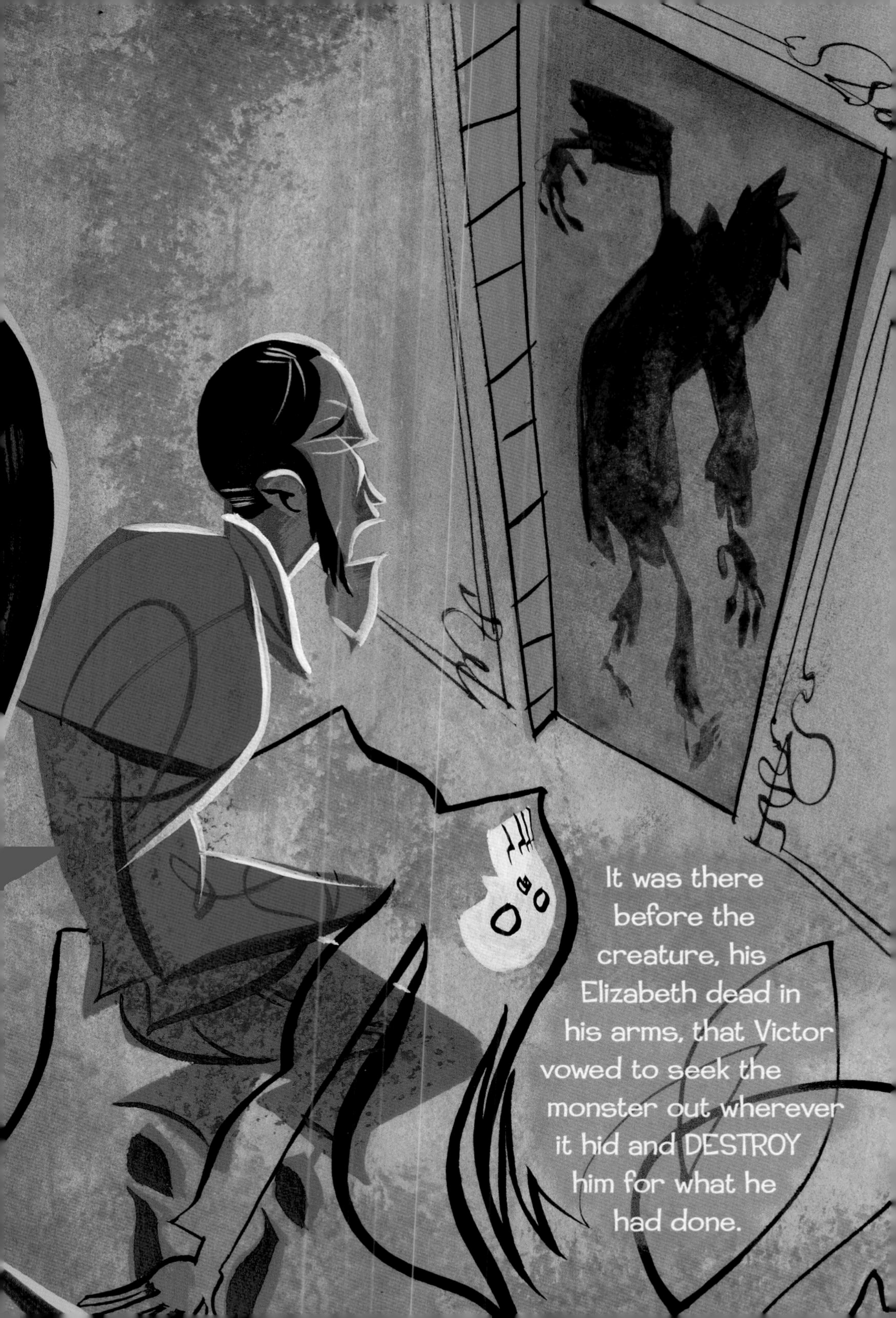
It was there before the creature, his Elizabeth dead in his arms, that Victor vowed to seek the monster out wherever it hid and DESTROY him for what he had done.

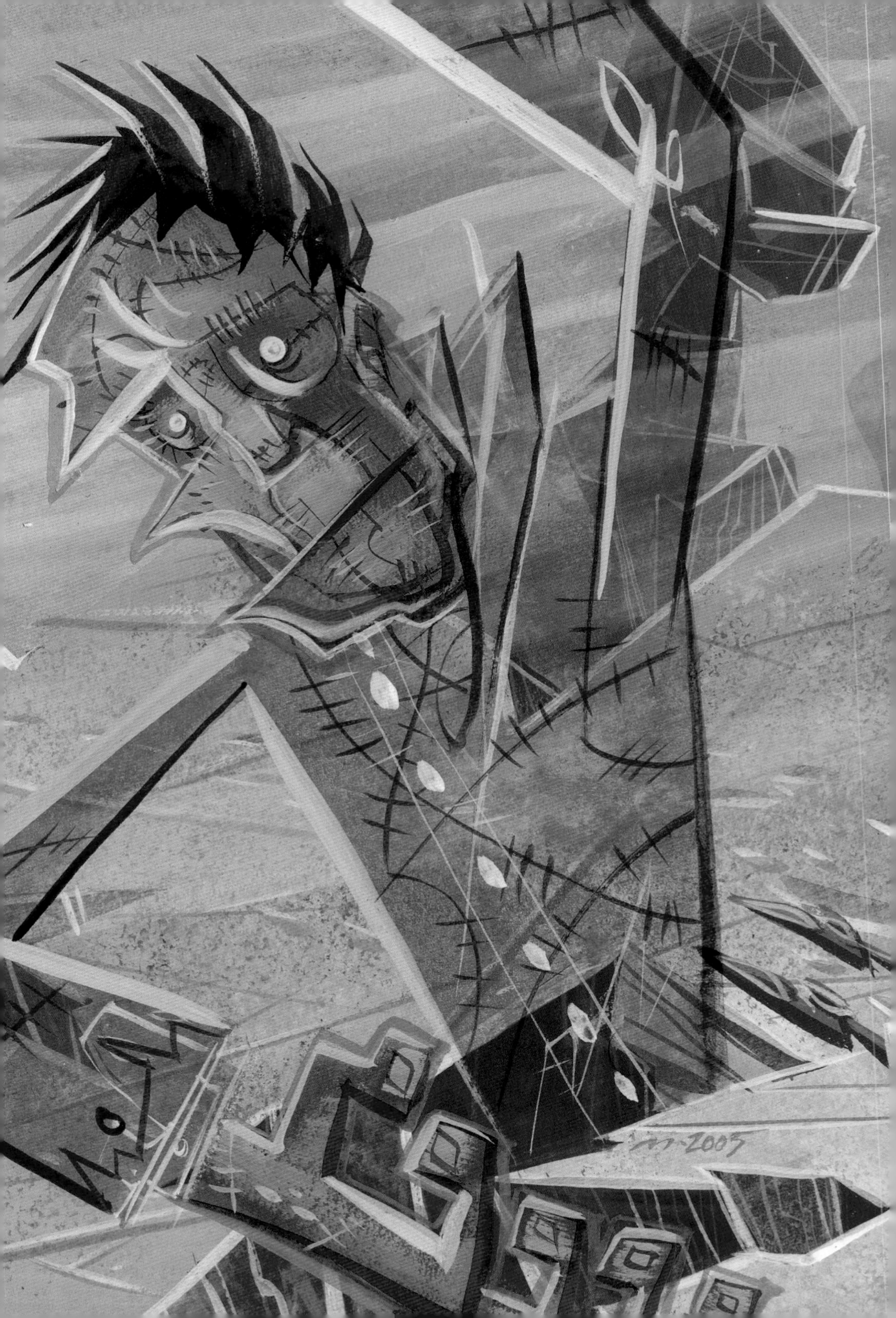

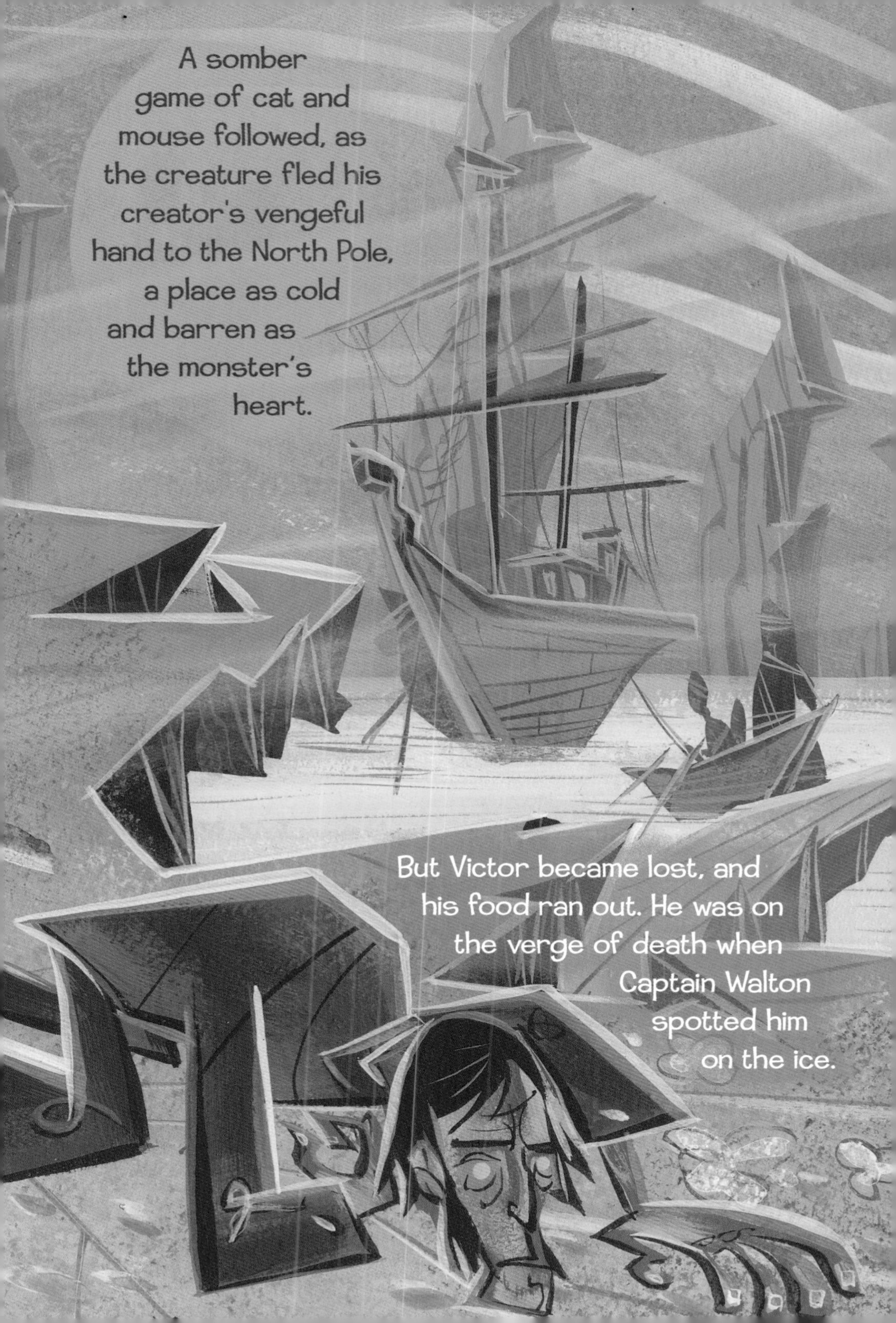

A somber game of cat and mouse followed, as the creature fled his creator's vengeful hand to the North Pole, a place as cold and barren as the monster's heart.

But Victor became lost, and his food ran out. He was on the verge of death when Captain Walton spotted him on the ice.

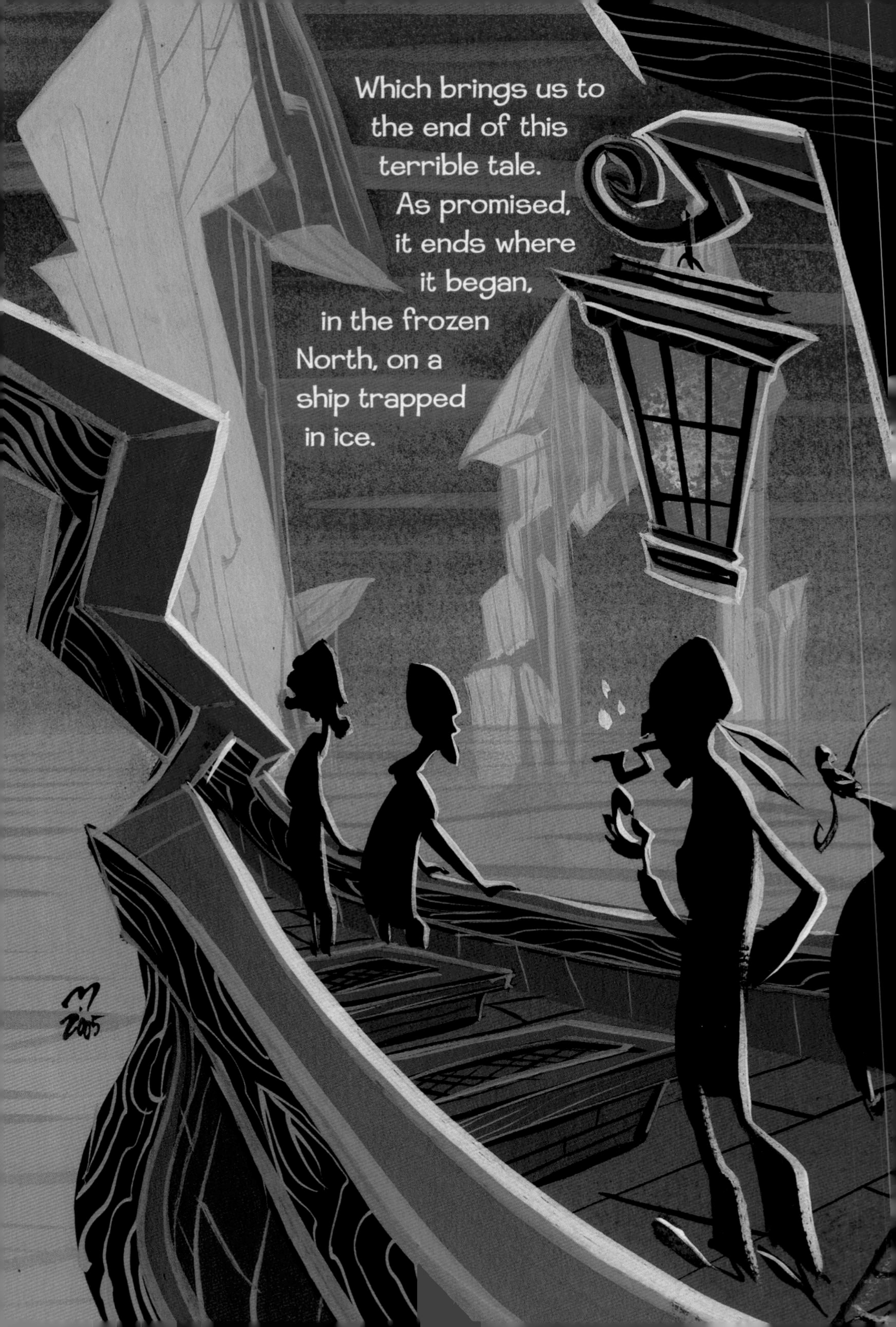
Which brings us to the end of this terrible tale.
As promised, it ends where it began, in the frozen North, on a ship trapped in ice.

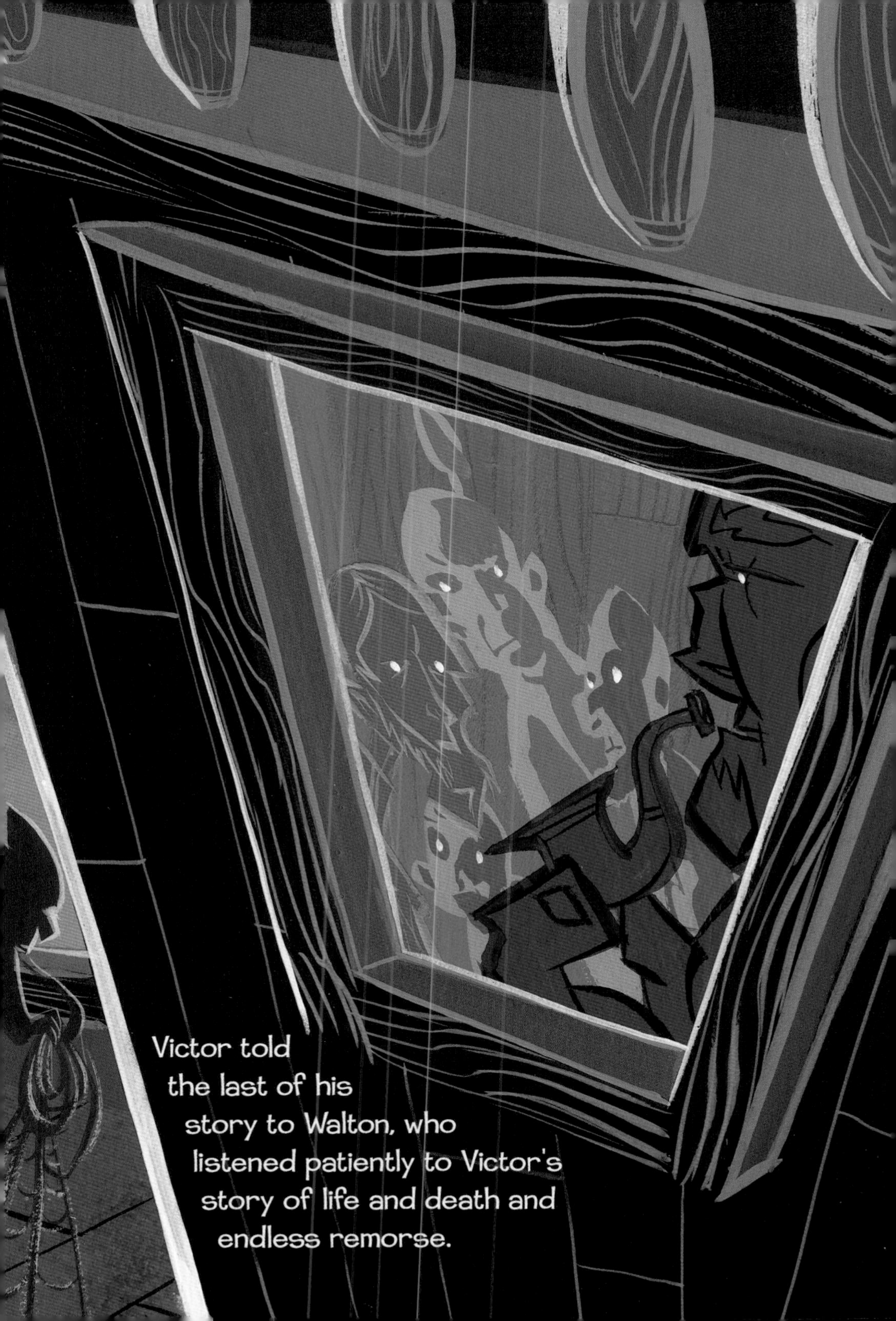

Victor told
the last of his
story to Walton, who
listened patiently to Victor's
story of life and death and
endless remorse.

And then, as if relieved of the burden of the account, Victor Frankenstein died, leaving Captain Walton to wonder if he had just heard the ranting of a madman. Not a word of what Frankenstein said could possibly be true!

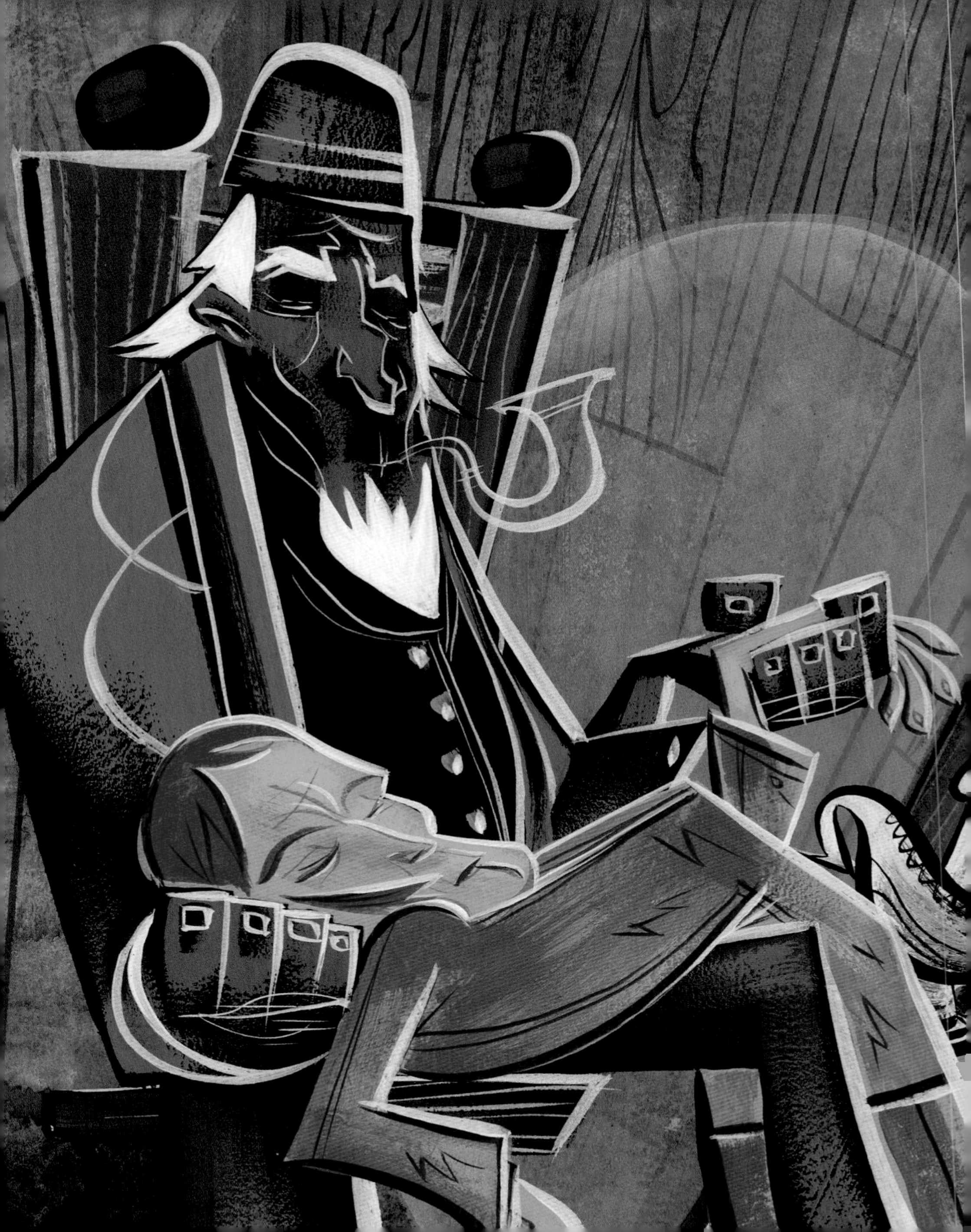

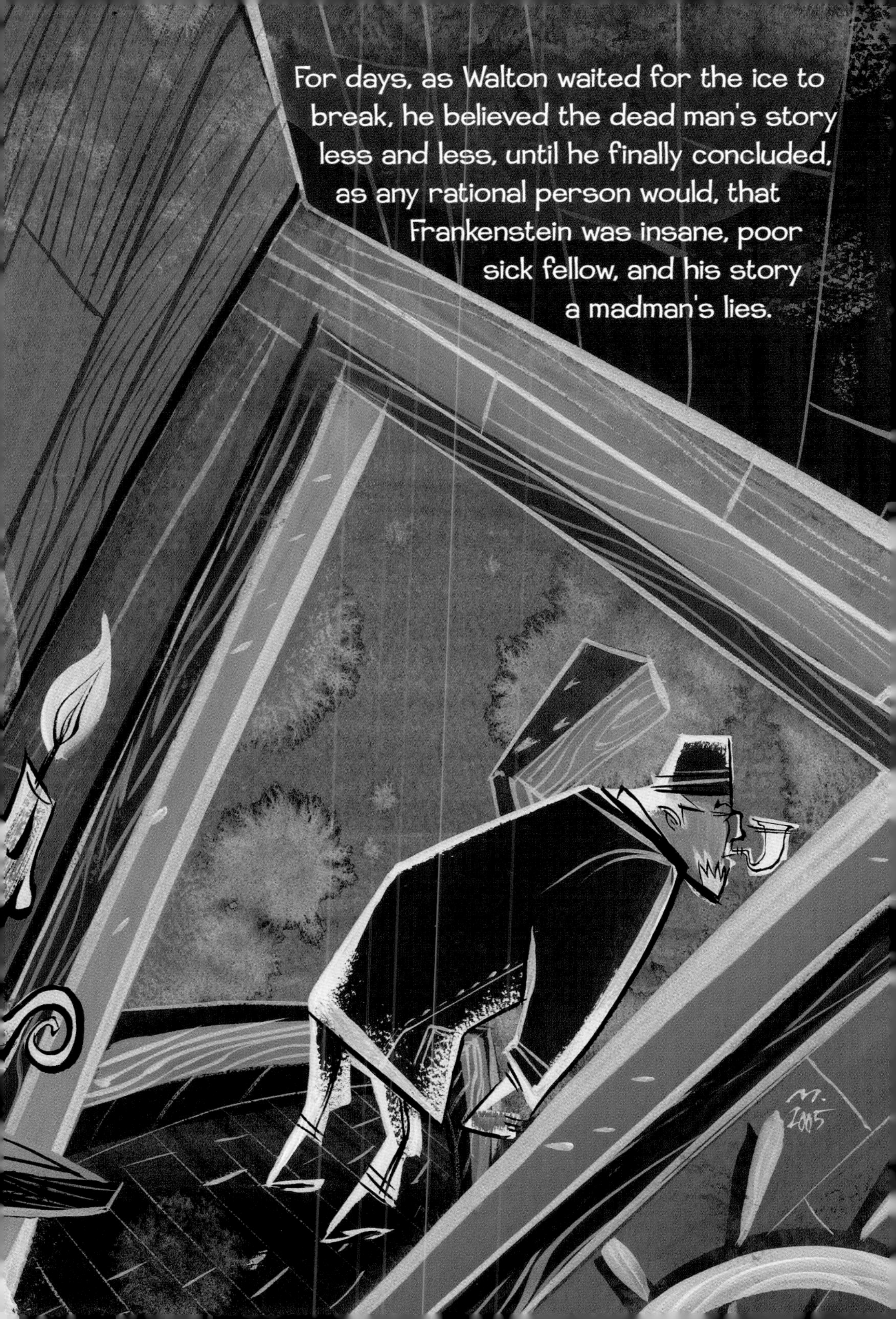
For days, as Walton waited for the ice to break, he believed the dead man's story less and less, until he finally concluded, as any rational person would, that Frankenstein was insane, poor sick fellow, and his story a madman's lies.
M. 2005

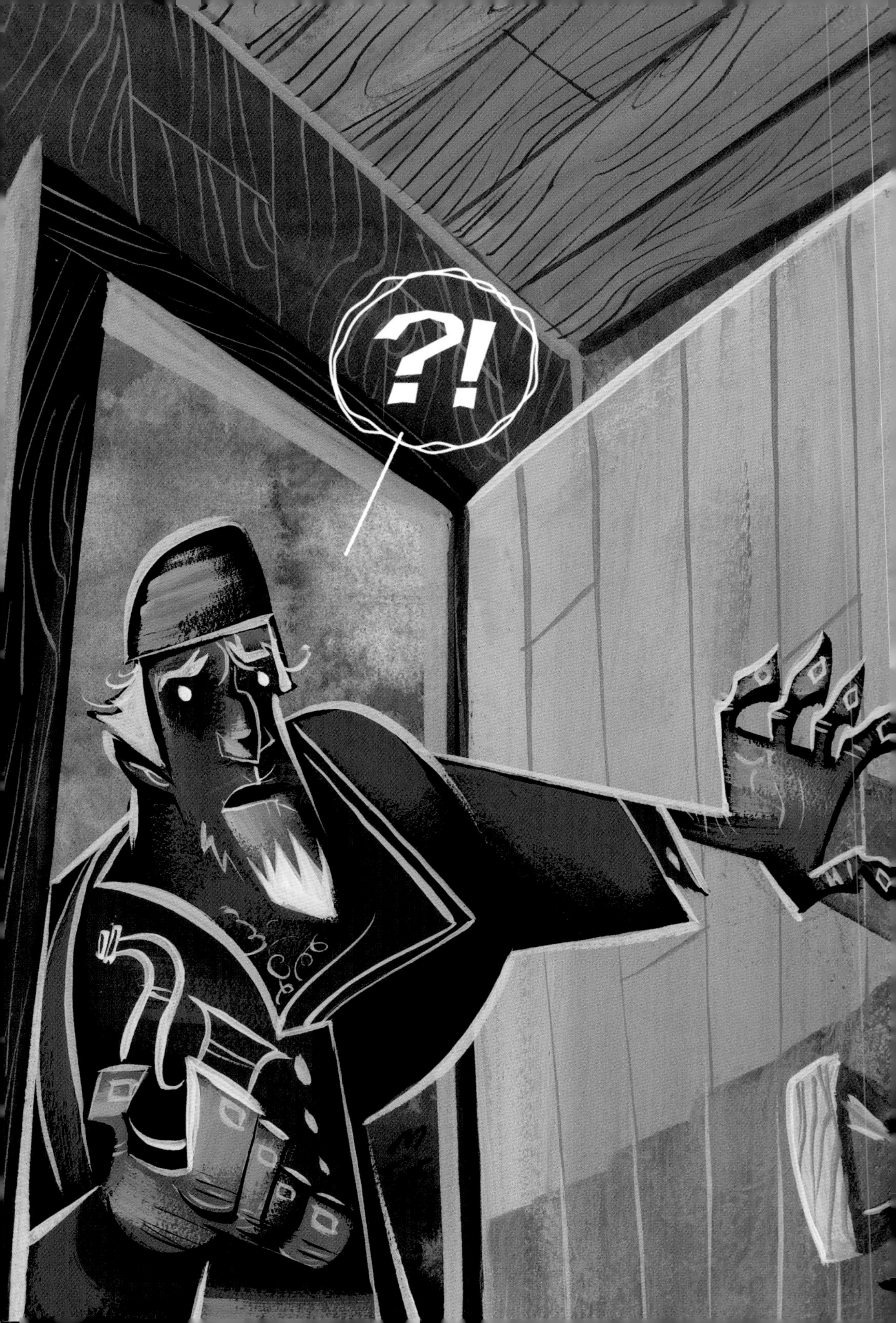
?!

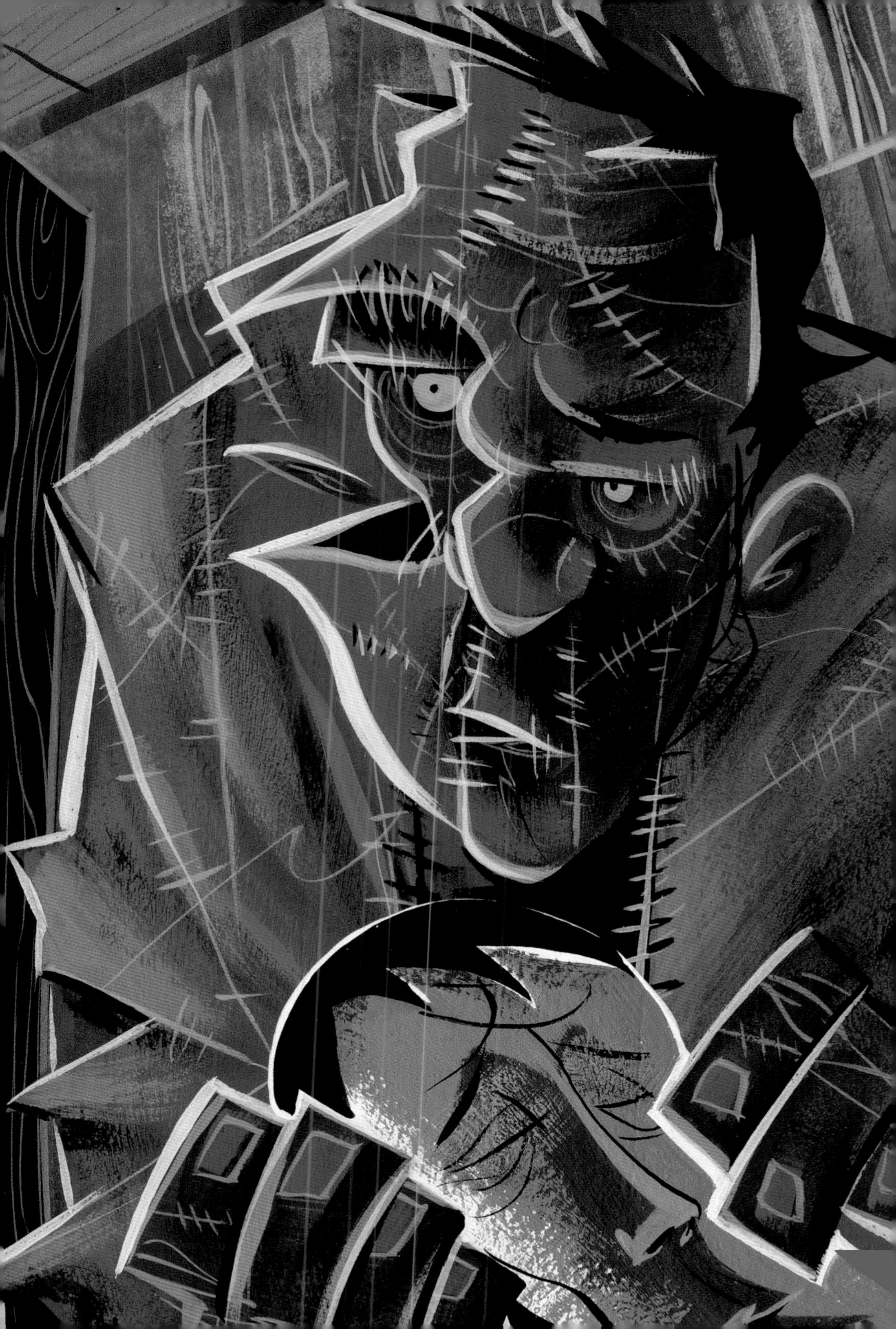

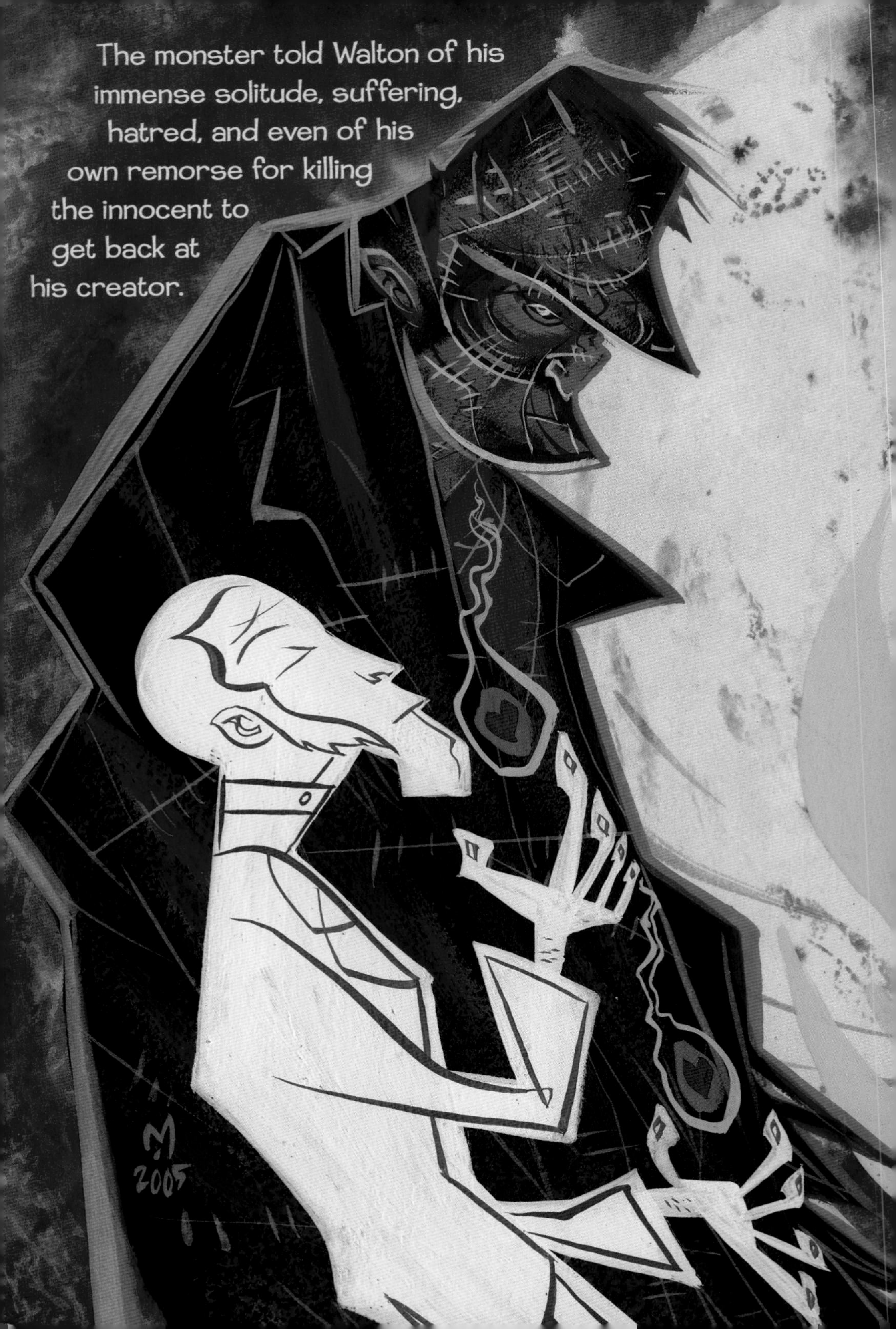
The monster told Walton of his immense solitude, suffering, hatred, and even of his own remorse for killing the innocent to get back at his creator.

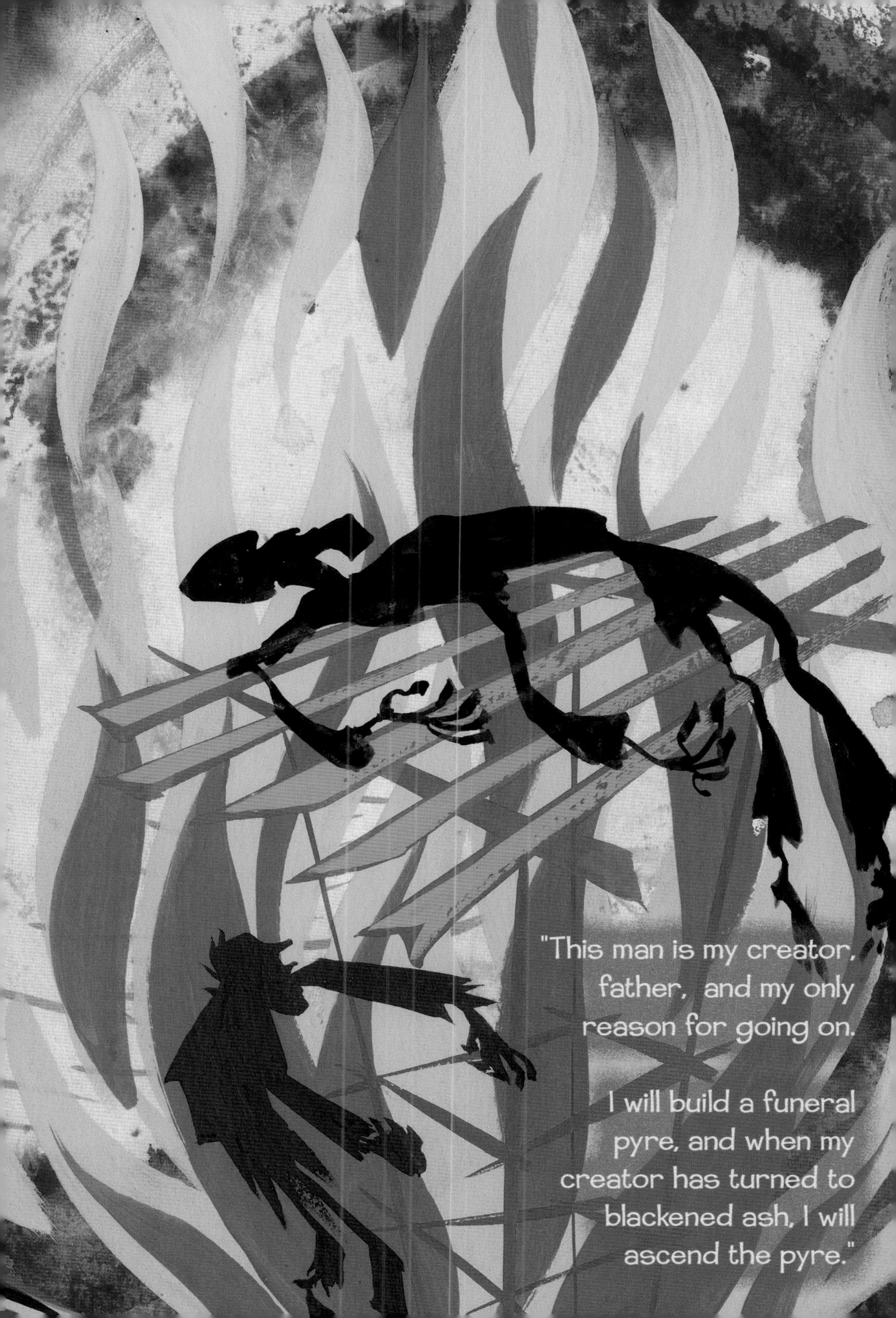

"This man is my creator, father, and my only reason for going on.

I will build a funeral pyre, and when my creator has turned to blackened ash, I will ascend the pyre."

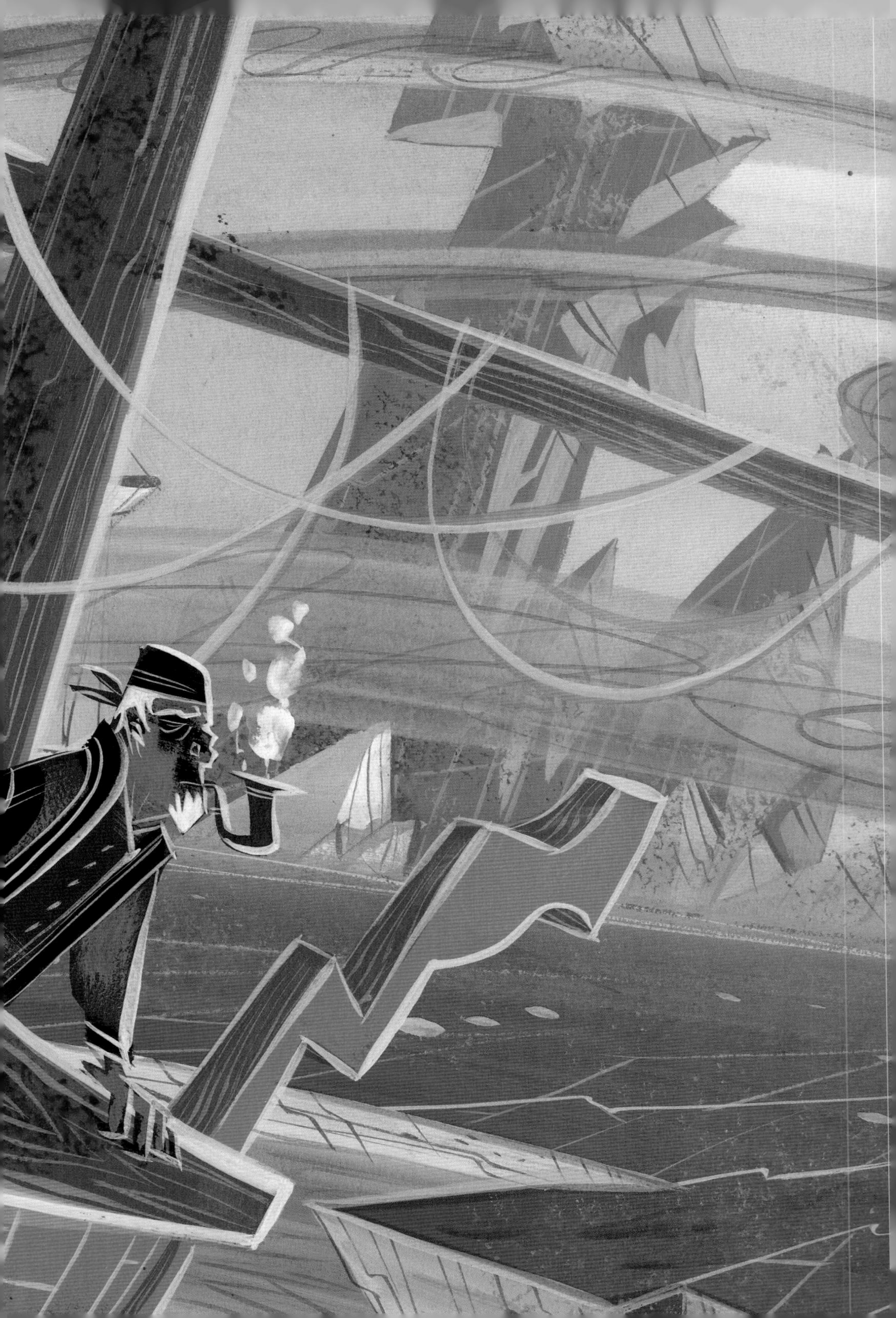

The monster then departed
for the northernmost ice,
never to be seen again.

THE END

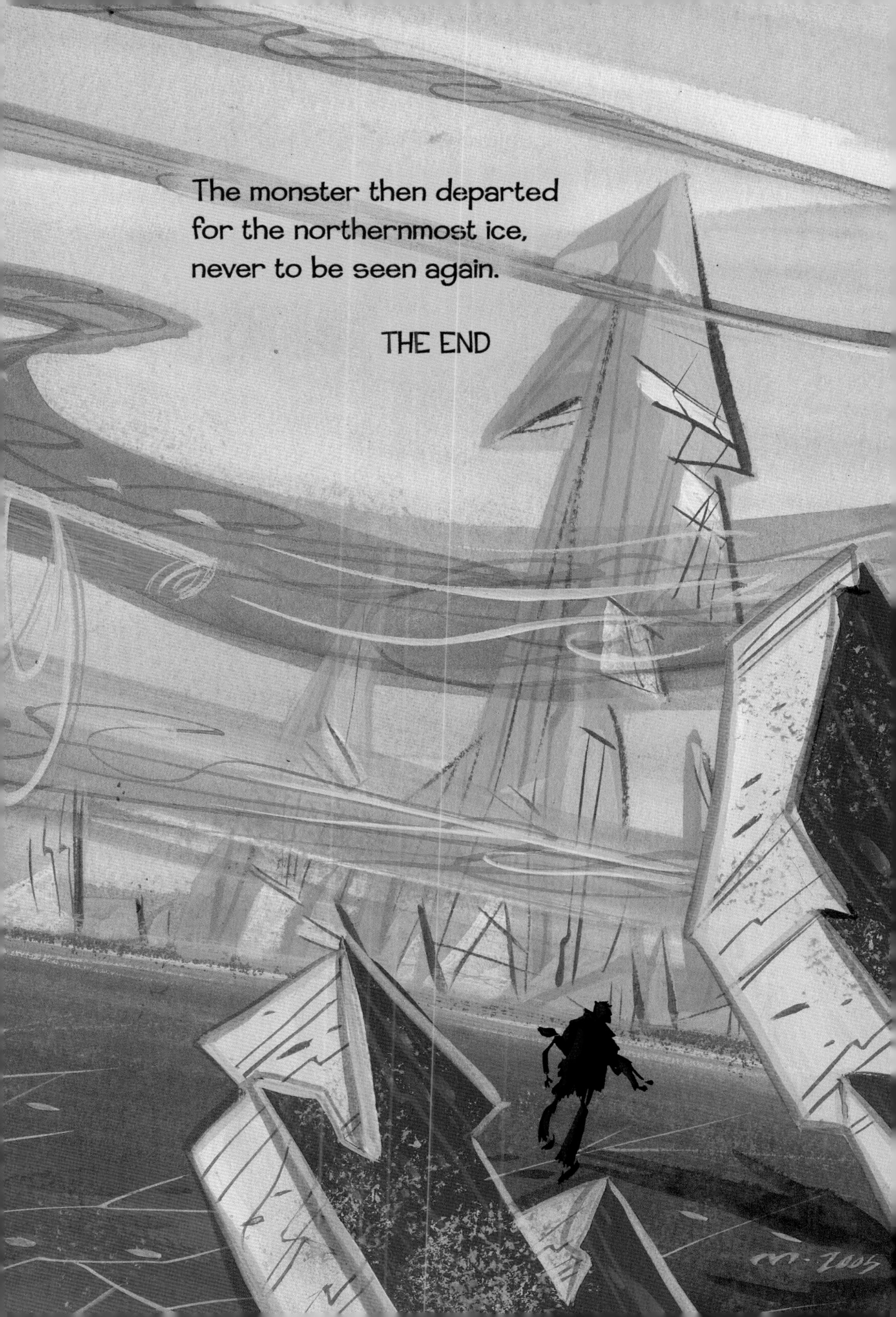

# STEVE NILES

STEVE NILES (www.steveniles.com) is one of the writers responsible for bringing horror comics back to the mainstream. Currently writing *Supernatural Freak Machine: A Cal McDonald Mystery, Bigfoot* (with Rob Zombie and Richard Corben), *30 Days of Night: Bloodsucker Tales,* and *American Freakshow* for IDW Publishing, Niles also has more Cal McDonald prose novels in the works and recently signed to write *30 Days of Night* prose novels as well.

2002's *30 Days of Night* comic is being developed as a major motion picture, with *Spider-Man 2*'s Sam Raimi producing. Also in production is a *Criminal Macabre* movie for which he will write the screenplay. Niles's *Wake the Dead* and *Hyde* have been optioned by Dimension Films, while Paramount Pictures has optioned the movie rights to *Aleister Arcane.*

Niles got his start in the industry when he formed his own publishing company called Arcane Comix, where he published, edited, and adapted several comics and anthologies for Eclipse Comics. His adaptations include works by Clive Barker, Richard Matheson, and Harlan Ellison. IDW released a hardcover collection of Niles's adaptation of Richard Matheson's *I Am Legend.*

Niles has a wide array of projects due in 2005, including *Bad Planet* (with Tom Jane), *Little Book of Horror: Dracula* (with artist Richard Sala), *Sacred Hearts, Earth vs. Monsters,* and more.

Niles lives in Los Angeles with his wife Nikki and their three black cats.

## SCOTT MORSE

SCOTT MORSE (www.scottmorse.com) is the award-winning creator of the graphic novels *Soulwind, The Barefoot Serpent, Southpaw, Spaghetti Western,* and others. In animation, his clients have included Universal, Cartoon Network, Disney, and most recently Nickelodeon, where he served as Art Director on the television series *Catscratch.* He's currently working full-time with Pixar and enjoying life with his family in Northern California.

## MARY SHELLEY'S *FRANKENSTEIN*

Written in 1816 when she was only nineteen, MARY SHELLEY's novel chillingly dramatized the dangerous potential of life begotten upon a laboratory table. A frightening creation myth for any era, *Frankenstein* remains one of the greatest horror stories ever written and is an undisputed classic of its kind.

*Frankenstein* has been reprinted, translated, abridged, and dramatized numerous times, with stage performances beginning as early as 1823. There have been multiple film versions and elaborations, as well as sequels and spoofs. But most of these takes deviate from Shelley's original tale, which played more as an update of the myth of Prometheus. The terror evoked by her original patchwork monster has been subsumed by a more romanticized version of the creature. IDW's *Little Book of Horror: Frankenstein* presents the creature, and the tale itself, as Shelley originally intended.

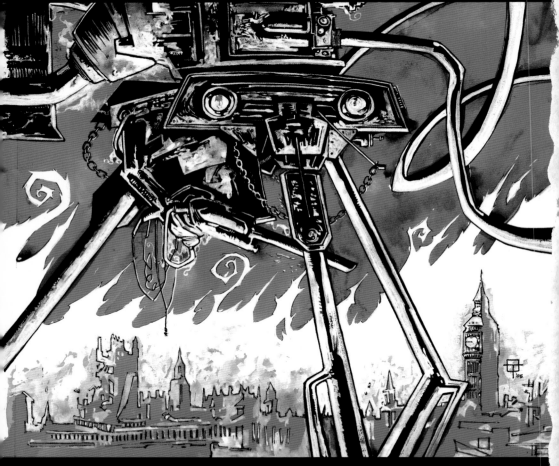

# LITTLE BOOK OF HORROR
## THE WAR OF THE WORLDS

COMING SUMMER 2005

STEVE NILES • TED McKEEVER

WWW.IDWPUBLISHING.COM